Straight 'A's in GCSE

MIND-MAP YOUR WAY TO EXAM SUCCESS

Ken Adams

D1354159

Thorsons
An Imprint of HarperCollins*Publishers*

Thorsons
An Imprint of HarperCollins*Publishers*
77–85 Fulham Palace Road,
Hammersmith, London W6 8JB
1160 Battery Street,
San Francisco, California 94111–1213

Published by Thorsons 1995
1 3 5 7 9 10 8 6 4 2

© Ken Adams 1995

Ken Adams asserts the moral right to
be identified as the author of this work

A catalogue record for this book
is available from the British Library

ISBN 0 7225 3039 0

Printed in Great Britain by Woolnough Bookbinding Limited
Irthlingborough, Northamptonshire

Contents

Preface

This is a book about strategies for learning. The following chapters will show you how to achieve high grades, including A* or Super A, in all the major GCSE subjects. Up-to-date principles of learning, including mind-mapping, relevant imaging and mnemonics, are used to show how the GCSE syllabus and attainment targets of the National Curriculum can be easily attained. Mind-maps are a way of organizing your learning into theme areas using key words, diagrams, mnemonics etc. (A fuller description follows in Chapter 1.) You are shown how it is possible to remember facts, principles and processes and how to problem-solve, using only recent examination material and actual course-work examples. The subject matter at GCSE level is exhaustively mind-mapped, for science and maths in particular, and the treatment of English is extensive.

The text shows you how, by effective imaging, you will *never forget*. You can then carry the ideas and principles from these pages forward to A levels and degree work.

How to use this book

This book is useful on several levels:

- **For reference**   The science and maths sections, in particular, provide a complete syllabus for GCSE. The areas are themed, and so can be used for quick referral for homework and assignment work. Much of the English and language areas are similarly useful. In English, spelling and grammar rules are laid out for ease of access.

- **As a revision manual**   When revising for module testing, for the mock exams and for the GCSE itself, this book is especially valuable. Learning, whether at a point remote from the exam or within a few days of it, should be within a theme. There are several points to consider.

Where a sequential series of facts, comments and quotations has to be remembered (as in English literature): start at '12 o'clock', trace along the 'start' line and *visualize* the starting events (create your own actions) and the quotations being used. Incorporate any comments about character, location etc. into your visualization. Move from this event, or series of events, to the second line and repeat the learning process. Visualization is best done against a 'back-drop' or by closing your eyes. Mnemonics should also be incorporated into your visualization exercise. Where events are sequential or related, an overall mnemonic to link them is invaluable. In order to effect memorization of 'patterns' of linking facts from within a theme, after visualization has been completed you will need to use the worked examples (which are up-to-date examination questions) and papers obtained from the Exam Board. Choose the questions which are testing your theme area and practise *dissection* and *re-assembly* techniques as detailed in the problem-solving and subject chapters. These, and the use of webs for brainstorming and mind-maps that you create for divergent problem-solving, will help you to 'read' the examiner's mind. At *all stages* creating a picture in your mind, whether by visualization, drawing diagrams or mapping, will create effective matching and allow you to 'build' in your mind.

Where items of information, processes and principles do *not* follow a sequence, related information along a line can be mnemonicized and visualized and then questions completed within this limited area. When the theme area has been exhaustively revised, the information can be 'pegged' by its position in the mind-map (relating to 'time' or 'compass direction' is very effective, for instance, Reproduction at N.E. on Life Process Map). The desire to 'move on quickly' has to be resisted. A little extra time spent on visualization and pegging will have immeasurable benefits in memorization and recall. Unlike 'cramming' just before an exam using notes, revision manual or textbook, the use of mind-maps *right up to the exam time* will only enhance recall. This is because use opens up the channels to the revised areas. Also, using the maps means a whole subject can be revised in fifteen minutes.

- **For assignments**   For maths and science, the practical and recording sequences should be followed carefully. 'Brainstorming' should be used to determine experimental paths to follow. Diagramming, use of graphs and other presentational devices are important, because the creation of clear visual images, in the mind of the marker, is as important as it is in revision. In the English section there is extensive information about the preparation of English assignments.

- **As a study skills and learning strategies manual**   Throughout the book there is extensive treatment of learning strategies. The book can

be read from this point of view alone; you may either use it as a
manual for *general* learning (the ideas apply to all learning in life in
general) or for learning within a specific subject area.

• **For computer programs**   One of the most important applications of
this book is in the production of computer disks for learning. A theme
area can quickly be transferred to a disk and the ends of the 'lines' put
into visual or animated form. You can 'attach' a series of examples
and questions to these specific areas with in-built *programmed learning*
to ensure proper understanding of key areas. This, in effect, is
mimicking the way the mind operates in learning. The implications of
these ideas for computerized learning cannot be under-estimated.
Textbook learning can be reduced from hundreds of pages to a score
of very simple files, and will also be *far more memorable*.

one

Learning for GCSE

The tall, 16-year-old student peered down at my small, 8-year-old son. 'How did you find the exam?' he asked. 'I couldn't do any of it!'

'Easy,' said John, with a grin (he passed with a good grade).

'Soon they'll be having 3-year-olds doing this exam,' said the tall boy.

It will probably happen one day. Age is no bar to *knowing*. Success in examinations is about memorizing facts, principles or concepts (like *pressure*) and processes (like how to *multiply*). It is also about knowing how to dissect and solve problems, how to set out an assignment or how to pull together related facts to create an essay. To attain these objectives you will need to *focus effectively* on what you need to learn by the organization of your work into easily digestible form.

This organization contributes to understanding and, with the aid of *pegs* or *mnemonics* of various kinds, will result in easy recall. This book will help you to achieve startling progress through the development of your abilities to *register*, *retain* and *recall* GCSE subject matter and so get good grades.

PROCESSING INFORMATION

Since memorization is the key to effective learning, the way that the mind processes information is of central importance.

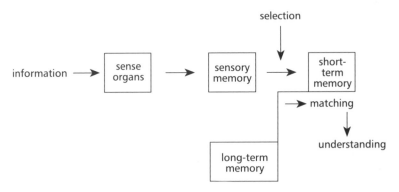

Whatever information you *scan* with your sense organs – and that includes eyes, ears, skin, nose, taste buds – is temporarily held (in coded form) by a sensory memory for a very short time. Selected information is then passed on to short-term memory which holds it for long enough to initiate a 'scan' of long-term memory. If the information creates a clear enough mental image (a kind of 'picture') it can then be matched with something similar to that in memory. Then, you understand what you are looking at; it has meaning.

Cramming

At this point, there are two things of vital importance. The first thing is that if too much information comes into short-term memory too quickly, earlier information is displaced. This means that there will then not be sufficient time for matching to occur. For this reason, it is best to *stagger* information. Trying to *cram* your learning results in losing information. Also, if the information presented to you cannot easily be visualized, then understanding and memorizing is difficult. The pages of many textbooks are like this: what has to be learnt is often submerged in text, overlong worded explanation or irrelevant pictures. When this happens, a student finds it difficult to separate *key information* from irrelevant and distracting information and this hinders *understanding* and *effective memorizing*.

Mental 'pictures'

Creating a mental picture of what you are learning is of vital importance. You can aid this process by creating in your mind pictures of 'concrete' items like the parts of a plant, or abstract ideas (concepts) like 'Force' (e.g. pictures of people pushing, pulling or hitting a golf ball) or of processes like transposing a formula in algebra, best seen as a factory machine digesting and operating on a variable (x):

$$2x + 2 = 8$$

is

$$x \longrightarrow \boxed{\times 2} \longrightarrow \boxed{+ 2} \longrightarrow 8$$

$$3 \longleftarrow \boxed{\div 2} \longleftarrow \boxed{- 2} \longleftarrow x = 3$$

reverse

The clearer the picture you create in your mind, the better are you able to match it with something in your memory.

Matching

The second, and equally important, aspect of scanning is that incoming information (what you are learning) must relate fairly closely to something already firmly entrenched in long-term memory. For example, in your memory you will have a generalized concept of a house.

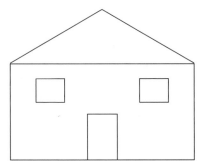

You will be able to produce an image (picture) of it in your mind and be able to draw it. It will probably look something like the simple drawing on the previous page. When you see an object that looks like a house, you have matched or superimposed the image of the real house on the image created in your mind. You have an *understanding* that this is a house. You then note any differences and link these differences (peg) to the place and time in which you saw it.

Sometimes you *think* you have a match; like a short-sighted man who thinks he sees a number 31 bus, runs like crazy and finds that it's a number 13, going the other way. This is a *mis-match* when you *mis-understand*. A *non-match* situation is illustrated by the Eskimo who, living in the deepest Arctic, has never seen a brick-built house and when faced by one for the first time would be totally bewildered as to its purpose.

This means that if you are learning GCSE work you must ensure that there is a good match or near match in memory. This contributes to so-called 'memory building'. In maths, for example, cancelling in fractions *cannot* be learnt before division. Much learning must be graded, stepwise, and if you do not understand something you may need to go back to 'basics'. In maths your knowledge is a giant network and, sometimes, if you try to learn something new, you can 'fall' into a hole where an item of knowledge is missing for you to build on.

BUILDING KNOWLEDGE IN MEMORY

Unusual, colourful and emotion-provoking images are very memorable and we learn by building 'oddities' into memory. This is a mechanism for survival because, when we meet something new, we need to understand it to decide whether it is safe or not. This new experience can be a perfect match with something in memory, in which case we will understand perfectly; but we do not learn anything. This might be one reason why there is such wide diversity in 'intelligence' between individuals. Some people remain in the same environment, not meeting new situations and challenges, whereas other people progress in respect to their mind building by solving problems and diversifying.

If the new experience is a *near-match* (for example, a cube can be recognized – not by word, but by *form* – as a 3-D form of a square), we build the new experience on to what is already in memory. We also understand. However, the new information is only available for easy recall if we *revise* it often (keep the mental channels open) or if it is *pegged* (attached to some extravagant image).

If the new experience does not match (for example, the Eskimo being shown a house) we do not link it effectively to anything in memory. It will link to something superficial, as when we are faced with some foreign hieroglyphics. Understanding then is of the mere form of the lines – it is *superficial understanding*.

This means that to learn anything properly, new information should be learned within 'theme' areas (areas of related knowledge). Then, the steps forward from knowing one thing to learning another are very short. Links between themes, linking algebra and area for example, can be made later through problem-solving.

Gradually, we move from knowing what a 'house' is to learning about different types of houses. Moving from the general to the specific, from 'house' to 'semi-detached', 'detached', 'cottage' and 'mansion', we move from 'tree' to 'oak', 'elm' and 'sycamore'. So:

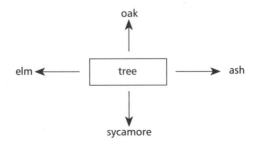

Or maybe:

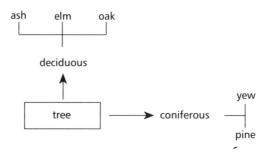

This is the mind-map form, and the way that we learn (how our minds work) is one reason why it is so effective.

Real life

Creating understanding and recalling information is directly related to the ability to match whatever you are learning with real-life experience. In trying, for example, to illustrate pressure by having an elephant standing on a giant drawing pin, you are trying to relate new information to the most firmly established, most used area of memory – that concerned with real-life experience. Concrete images are always remembered better than abstract ones because *all* knowledge is built on early experience of the world.

This means that you need to translate abstract items or concepts into concrete images, so that a good match with real-life experience is made. Make up stories about whatever you wish to learn because real life is a story itself, full of countless sub-plots. The story form is very effective in making for easy recall, for example, 'The Old Arab Sat On His Camel And Hiccuped' for trigonometry. This is a 'peg' on which to hang the concepts of this particular aspect of maths. All knowledge can be processed by relevant imaging, although this needs a little application. This book does a lot of the work for you.

PREPARATION

The paragraphs above are about what takes place *within* the mind. Adequate preparation of what you wish to learn *before* it enters your sense organs can *greatly* enhance learning.

Filing

Long-term memory is a highly complex filing system. When we try to retrieve information we are searching at tremendous speed, scanning labels, withdrawing files and trying to find perhaps one item. Memory is like an enormous filing cabinet, with many labelled drawers of related information containing files of even more closely related items. (The simile is slightly imperfect, however, because, ostensibly, cross-connections between files and unrelated items are possible.) How much easier it is to find what you are looking for if:

a the drawers and files are clearly marked
b both drawers and files contain closely related information, and
c there is a 'manageable' number of items in each file and drawer.

MIND-MAPS

These principles underpin the idea of breaking down information, processes and concepts into essential key themes, words, pictures or diagrams by abstracting unnecessary and distracting words etc. A central theme or concept is used to dominate subsidiary information, as can be seen overleaf. Setting out academic notes in this form (sometimes called a *mind-map*) is something our minds try to do anyway when we are learning in the 'traditional' way. However, because of the amount of distracting information in a textbook, the mind finds it difficult to produce clear images for matching. Hence, learning is limited. Setting out key words and ideas into a map of easily digestible size makes for ease of filing. Also, the pattern of branching from one central generalized concept to more specific related ideas is very clear.

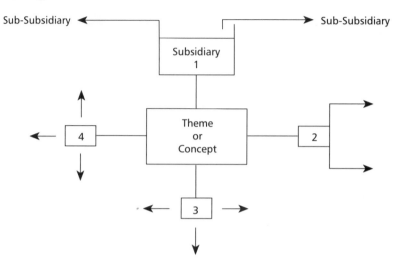

Another reason for such a format being of great use for learning is that the layout of a mind-map is like the layout of a real map, especially the sort that we create every day of our lives when we plan our journeys to school, college or work – we go down this road, turn left, then right and so on. It is also like another real-life image that we encounter every single day – that of the clock. In creating mind-maps, telling stories and translating abstract information into concrete mental pictures, we are linking to real-life experience through well-used channels.

Mental images and pictures

Once all your work is laid out for easy filing in memory, each word or concept, principle or process, has to be clearly translated for understanding into mental pictures. Mnemonics, creating 'peg pictures' in the mind, complete the process to give easy recall. Pictures, diagrams and cartoons are preferable to words. (See mind-map opposite.)

All information as mental pictures

Ultimately the key to the whole process is in creating mental pictures of *all* information, whether in science, maths, English or languages. That we can easily learn to do this is illustrated by our learning of real-life

```
┌──────────┐     ┌──────────┐     ┌──────────┐     ┌──────────┐
│ learning │     │ put into │     │  mind-   │     │individual│
│ material │ ──▶ │  themes  │ ──▶ │   map    │ ──▶ │ items as │
│          │     │          │     │          │     │ pictures │
│          │     │          │     │          │     │ diagrams │
│          │     │          │     │          │     │or cartoon│
└──────────┘     └──────────┘     └──────────┘     └──────────┘
                                                          │
                                                          ▼
                                          ┌──────────────────────────┐
                                          │ make mnemonics where      │
                                          │ concrete images do not    │
                                          │ readily spring to mind    │
                                          └──────────────────────────┘
```

experience. For example, if you go to a new street in a new town, for
some time afterwards you will be able to remember very clearly aspects
of that street even though you have made *little or no effort* to remember.
This is because from birth you have had to memorize real-life experience ad hoc (if only for survival). In our minds we have a generalized
concept of 'a street' – pavement, shops or houses, lampposts, roadway,
etc. When you encounter a new street you notice idiosyncrasies (oddities) of that particular street and plug these into the general concept.
You then 'peg' these oddities for easy recall into time and place. You
went to that street, for example, between 2.00p.m. and 3.00 p.m. on 31st
March 1995. When you wish to recall you simply track through your
time and *place* files, link up to the *street* file, identify the new street and
recreate its image. Such principles of learning have been adapted in this
book to both the concrete and abstract knowledge in GCSE. The mind-
maps in science and maths, in particular, are presented so that
processes and principles are in image-provoking forms (patterns).

PROBLEM-SOLVING

There are other aspects of GCSE that need to be considered. One is
problem-solving, which is considered in more detail in the next
chapter. In GCSE, problem-solving is at the core of the exams and
course-work. It is basically of two types: convergent and divergent
problem-solving.

Convergent problem-solving comes up with single answer. The problem
has to be *dissected* out into subsidiary problems and these have to be

solved before an answer can be produced. Mind-mapping is very useful for facilitating this. Several items, or processes, are separated into a mind-map and *new* links made to solve the problem.

Divergent problem-solving is increasingly becoming part of GCSE, especially in biology. It is very like creativity – brainstorming for ideas related to the problem (question) in hand and linking them. A typical example might be, 'What are the benefits to an earthworm of living in a wood?'

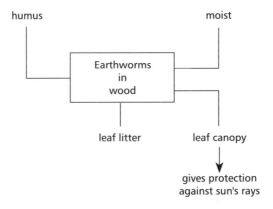

Assignments in science and maths also have this creative element.

SKILLS

Skills have to be practised, too. Certain processes in mathematics and science need to be so firmly embedded in memory that time is not wasted in the middle of an examination trying to remember basics. One of the commonest failings in otherwise proficient maths students is confusion over simple manipulative skills. I am continually asked, often in the middle of working out a high-level maths problem, 'What does (– × –) give?' or, 'What happens when I divide 3 by two-thirds?' It is not enough to be able merely to understand a process. When learning to drive a car, for example, you could probably get along in a lonely country road by recalling successive operations visualized from a driving manual. However, for driving in a busy town centre, such skills should have been learnt to the point where they are instinctive. Similarly, you will not be able to unravel the complexities of problem solving successfully when you are distracted by the basics.

Making practice effective

There are certain fundamentals involved in practice:

a Of a list of related facts, or a process, the beginnings and ends are frequently remembered better than the middle. It is therefore good policy to concentrate on the middle of the list or process when learning. Simply raise your level of concentration 'in between'.
b Research has shown that the longer you leave a new subject unrevised the more difficult it is to relearn.

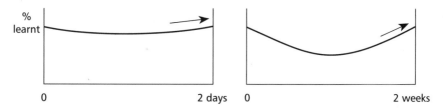

To revise and retain as much as possible it is best that you have:

• the first relearning session after about 2 days
• the second session after 2 weeks
• the third session after 2 months.

c Practice need not be done on paper or in the 'real' world. Professional musicians are famed for their ability to practise concertos in their heads. This is called 'rehearsal' and, obviously, can be enacted anywhere and without equipment of any kind. In academic work it also constitutes superior practice, because in doing it this way you *have* to produce clear mental pictures. Rote learning is long winded and relatively ineffective, because it creates only superficial mental images and takes much longer for memorizing. Similarly, mindlessly reading over your notes for hour after hour results in very poor learning. You will need understanding, and recall, at your fingertips.

ASSOCIATED FACTORS FOR LEARNING

Motivation

There are two further factors that could scupper all your efforts to achieve good grades. First, you must be *well-motivated* to learn. This can be a reaching for long-term objectives, like a good job or further study; or you could set yourself shorter-term objectives like achieving good grades to please parents or, in the spirit of good competitiveness, to do better than friends (or enemies). They are, essentially, rewards for your effort and you will need to focus on them by dreaming a little – about a job that fills you with self-importance, is satisfying or worthwhile or that simply is going to provide you with money. The future 'Mr Universe' works on his ambition by putting up a picture of Arnold Schwarzenegger in his work-out room. He is not so much motivated by his enjoyment of the repetitious exercise, but by the image of the perfect body that floats before his eyes. Similarly, you need to dangle a carrot before your eyes – especially when the work is boring and rigorous.

It has also been found that study is more effective if you break after approximately three-quarters of an hour to stretch your legs or have a cup of coffee and a biscuit. The break is a *reward* that you can look forward to while working. You can tell yourself that if you do not have the break your concentration will diminish and so your work will be less effective. This self-hypnosis will enhance the motivating effort of the break.

Environment

Motivation can achieve the desired effect, resulting in the *concentration* that is needed to drive information into memory. But there must be minimal distraction and the second factor needed to ensure good learning is a relaxing atmosphere. Humour relaxes and it is a useful maxim that a two-minute laugh will relax you for almost an hour. The wise teacher relaxes students with a short, humorous introduction to learning time; and it will help you immeasurably if you can lay your hands on something humorous when you break or just before you begin a learning session.

Apart from this you have to find the conditions under which you work best. The surroundings which suit one person will not suit another. Some people work best in a quiet room; others need background music. Also, your mood will vary from day to day. Ultimately, however, the stronger your motivation the less the working environment will matter.

SUMMARY

The material that you need to learn must be reduced to concrete, pictorial form so that it can be understood. For memorizing and recall, *mind-maps* and *mnemonics* are invaluable because they can make knowledge unforgettable. Certain skills should be practised to the point at which they become instinctive. This includes the practice of problem-solving, because patterns and strategies are also memorized.

Things can be memorable or well understood. In learning for GCSE you will want to achieve both memorability *and* understanding. The conditions for learning must be encouraging and there must be a high level of motivation in order that good concentration is achieved. When you are learning well, you begin to have confidence in your ability to *think*. You will realize that the professor who pontificates from the podium has learnt well – but may have had no more potential than you. The matter is in your hands: whereas chemistry tells us that matter can neither be created nor destroyed, by contrast intelligence can either be nurtured (created) or neglected (destroyed). Now it is up to you.

two

Problem-solving in GCSE

At the root of GCSE is problem-solving. Faced with a problem, the GCSE student looks for a pattern to recognize. If the solution is not obvious, time is spent finding a pattern. This sort of time-span is available when you are given a science assignment, or maths course-work, but in an exam knowledge of the typical patterns of exam problems needs to be at your finger-tips. Sometimes nowadays, particularly in maths and science, divergent thinking is also required which results in several answers, although these problems are usually simple.

RIGID THINKING

The number of problem patterns in GCSE maths and science are limited (these are dealt with fully in other chapters). This means that practice with core problems can make a student very flexible in recognizing exam patterns. The problem that occurs less frequently, requiring totally original thinking, can be catered for by developing the ability to break away from conventional or 'circular' thinking. This will need confidence in your own ability to be able to ignore rigid rules and 'free-think'.

Rigid thinking is illustrated by the way that a famous maze was developed. You are told to start at the entrance to this maze (on the outside) and find your way to the centre. Naturally, we have learnt throughout

our lives that in order to get somewhere we *aim* for that place. Therefore, in trying to get to the centre of the maze everyone takes the
turning that appears to lead to the centre. The planners who built the
maze were well aware of people's habitual thinking and arranged
things so that the more people turned towards the centre the more they
were doomed to the outer passages. The trick is to ignore your natural
inclination and instead aim to get to the *outside*. In so doing you eventually find yourself at the *centre*. Coming back, you reverse thinking
and your path.

LATERAL THINKING

Examiners are also aware of the habitual nature of GCSE students'
thinking. Thus, in maths papers, very strong students can be duped by
the obvious. For example, right in the middle of quite complex trigonometry questions a device is introduced that 'throws' many a student.
(Remember that distraction is also a device much used by stage magi-
cians to deflect the audience's attention from the main action.) So:

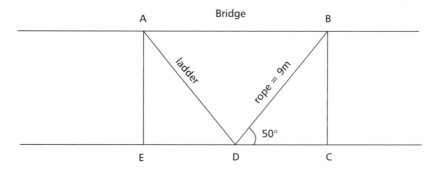

You are asked to find the length of BC, of CD and then ED, when AB is
10m. Everyone sails on, works out BC and CD using sine and cosine,
and then comes to a grinding halt at ED. This is because AB and CE are
visualized as 'removed' by the complexities in between. You are
distracted by the 'rope', for example, asking yourself, 'What on earth is
that needed for?' Later questions demand its use, but in the meantime
the simple subtraction, AB minus CD, is missed. What you need in

your memory is the *realization* that this particular aspect of the trigonometry problem may be there:

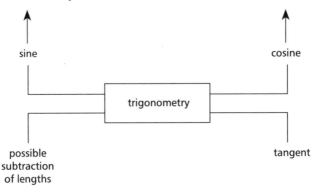

Eventually, when the examiner finds that such an element no longer confuses students, it will be removed because it will not be a 'test' anymore. However, distraction is and will be tried in problems as long as such things exist. It is apparently a fundamental failing of human nature to trip over the 'red herring'.

The need to think in a so-called *lateral* direction as opposed to the *vertical* is well summed up by Edward de Bono:

> Lateral thinking is made necessary by the limitations of vertical thinking. The terms 'lateral' and 'vertical' were suggested by the following considerations: it is not possible to dig a hole in a different place by digging the same hole deeper.
>
> Logic is the tool that is used to dig holes deeper and bigger, to make them altogether better holes. But if the hole is in the wrong place, then no amount of improvement is going to put it in the right place. No matter how obvious this may seem to every digger, it is still easier to go on digging in the same hole than to start all over again in a new place. Vertical thinking is digging the same hole deeper; lateral thinking is to try again elsewhere.
>
> *(Edward de Bono, 1967)*

To 'dig elsewhere' is an important strategy in problem-solving. It applies to aspects of convergent (one answer) problems as well as to divergent (many answer) problems. In addition to learning the strategies and patterns involved in specific subject problem-solving, you will need to learn how to create your own strategies. Below is a series of activities that should build up your ability to break habits of rigid thinking. Beware! Do not reject answers because they seem foolish!

Problem 1

Cut the cake below into *eight* pieces using *three* cuts only.

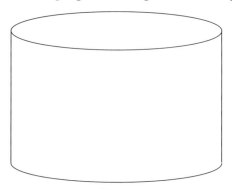

Note: there are several possible answers to this.

Good crossword puzzles can develop lateral thinking. A clue such as, 'What some pigeons do is sweet, they say (4)' leads you to think of jam or honey. But the clue is solved by knowing that pigeons *home* and there is home, *sweet* home.

Convergent thinking

'River-crossing' exercises are very popular. They can be made simple or complicated.

Problem 2: river crossing (simple)
Participants – 3 gorillas (GGG)
          – 3 monkeys (MMM)

There must *never* be more gorillas than monkeys on a river bank. The boat can carry no more than *two* at a time and all must get from the *left* river bank to the *right*, The gorillas and monkeys *in* the returning boat need not alight:

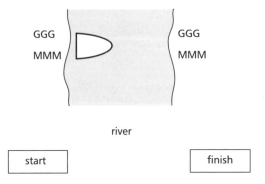

river

| start | | finish |

Problem 3: river crossing (more difficult)

This is identical to the above, but the animals in the boat *must always* alight when they reach a river bank, even if they return to it. This creates additional difficulty with numbers on the banks.

It is wise to record the trips diagrammatically. Answers are given at the end of the chapter.

Brainstorming

A problem with several possible answers requires you to brainstorm. The following are typical of some geography and science problems.

Problem 4: where to build a factory?

Your company wishes to open a factory to make television sets. The factory, which will employ 500 people, will import some parts from abroad and other parts will be made on site; many of the television sets will be exported.

You must select one of the sites, 1, 2, 3 or 4, and make a list of the reasons why you chose this site. Details of the sites:

Site 1   Six miles from the town centre, in the countryside and within

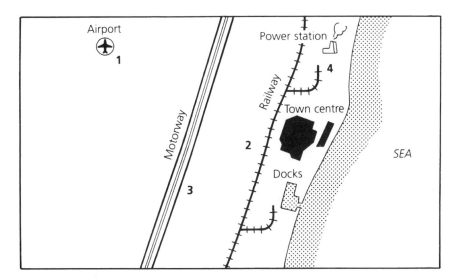

one mile of the airport. About two miles from the motorway. Rent and
rates quite low.

Site 2   About 2½ miles from the town centre and close to the docks.
Very close to the railway and about two miles from the motorway. Rent
and rates quite high.

Site 3   Very close to the motorway and four miles inland from the
coast. Two miles from the railway and about 3½ miles from the town
centre. Rent and rates reasonable.

Site 4   One mile from the town centre and close to the power station.
About 2½ miles from the docks, one mile from the railway and three
miles from the motorway. Rent and rates high.

When you are opening a factory there are lots of things to consider. For
example, are there enough skilled people nearby? How do we get the
parts to the factory?

Problem 5: building a dam
The regional water authority has decided to construct a dam across a

beautiful valley not far from where you live. You and most of the local population are annoyed and decide to fight against this decision.

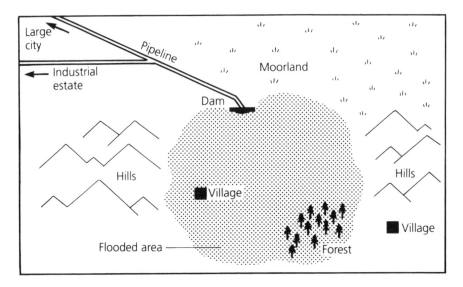

What arguments will you put forward against the dam being built there? Make a list.

TESTING A RULE

This is the basis of many science and maths assignments. The following problem illustrates the type of thinking that is needed to test a hypothesis (the rule that you believe applies to a particular problem). There is an element of trial and error about this type of problem-solving, but logic underpins your explanation of what you observe.

Problem 6: rule testing

The situation: four cards are presented, two have symbols (circle and triangle) and two have numbers (one odd and one even).

The rule: if a card has a circle on one side then it has an even number on the other side.

How can the rule be tested by turning over only two cards? Which cards would be turned over and why?

Testing 'hypotheses'

The following is a list of testable hypotheses. See if you can think of experiment you could set up to test such hypotheses.

- A rubber band can be used to weigh things.
- Magnetism will not pass through water.
- Wet paper is weaker than dry paper.
- Sound does not pass through water.
- Hair can be stretched.
- Some materials absorb more water than others.
- Objects float more easily in very salty water than in fresh water.

In each case it is a good idea to follow the general format:

1 State the hypothesis.
2 Set up an experiment to test it by varying one of the conditions (e.g. weight of rubber).
3 Set out a table of results.
4 Draw a graph of the results.
5 Comment on the graph.
6 State the rule that applies in this case.
7 Deduce any general rule that can be applied.
8 See if you can vary the experiment by adding a second condition (e.g. vary the thicknesses of rubber bands).

Specific assignments are dealt with in more detail in the different subject chapters, but the layout of an assignment should follow this general plan when the aim is to come up with a general rule (an algebraic equation, usually).

Initially, when faced with a long assignment, brainstorm:

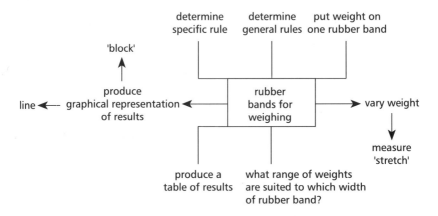

Answers to problems
Problem 1

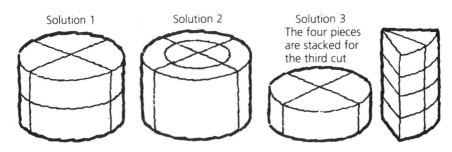

Solution 1   Solution 2   Solution 3
The four pieces
are stacked for
the third cut

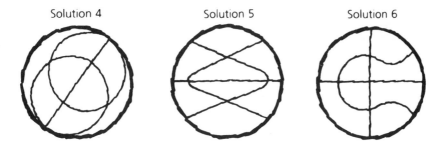

The following solution divides the cake into *ten* pieces using only three cuts.

Problem 2

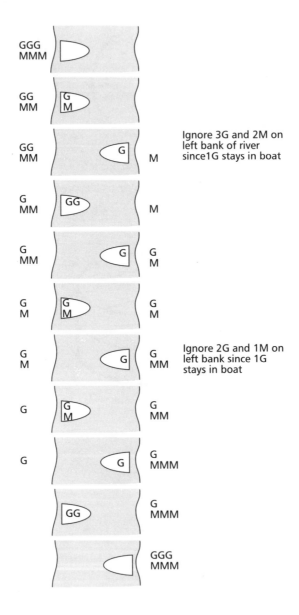

Ignore 3G and 2M on left bank of river since 1G stays in boat

Ignore 2G and 1M on left bank since 1G stays in boat

Problem 3

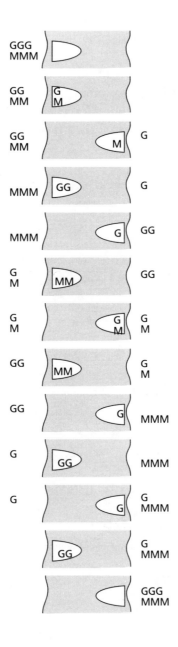

Problems 4 and 5

These problems show so-called divergent problem-solving and many 'right' answers are therefore possible.

Problem 6

This exercise can be quite difficult for adults and younger students may well not be able to grasp the logic. However, if sufficient time is given to reflection and discussion then it should be possible for most students to understand the basic concepts.

1 If card $\boxed{O}$ is turned over, and an even number is on the other side, then this substantiates the rule. If an odd number is on the other side then this goes counter to the rule. Card $\boxed{O}$ helps to test the rule.

2 If card $\boxed{\triangle}$ is turned over then this provides no evidence either to support or go counter to the rule. The rules says nothing about a $\boxed{\triangle}$ card but only refers to $\boxed{O}$. A $\boxed{\triangle}$ card can have an odd or even number on its reverse side.

3 If card $\boxed{6}$ is turned over and a circle is on the other side then this appears to substantiate the rule. If, however, a triangle is there then this in no way contradicts the rule. As mentioned in (2), a $\boxed{\triangle}$ card can have odd or even numbers on its reverse side. Turning over $\boxed{6}$ provides no test for the rule.

4 If card $\boxed{5}$ is turned over and a $\boxed{\triangle}$ is seen then this supports the rule, since a $\boxed{O}$ should not be observed. If a $\boxed{O}$ is seen, then this goes counter to the rule. Turning over $\boxed{5}$ helps test the rule.

In summary, cards $\boxed{O}$ and $\boxed{5}$ will test the rule.

It is most important to have a clear idea of what the rule is actually stating and not what your own interpretation may be.

SUMMARY

There are two basic types of problem-solving, divergent (many answers) and convergent (one answer). You will need to learn the strategies for solving these, particularly those of the type that GCSE examiners set. To be able to think laterally, and to use brainstorming techniques and mind-maps to solve problems, are invaluable tools. It is necessary to free yourself from rigid thinking techniques and the idea that there is always a definite answer to a problem. It is an important principle of problem-solving that, to initiate the thinking process, *something* related to the problem must be set down on paper – especially if it is in diagrammatic, mind-map or picture form.

three

GCSE science

The physics, chemistry and biology in this chapter is laid out for learning in mind-map form and there are extensive mnemonics of facts, principles and processes. The content is based on National Curriculum guidelines and on the GCSE board syllabuses for science (dual), science (single) and physics, chemistry and biology (separate subjects). The science mind-maps start on page 44 and are followed by the worked examples (exam papers) on page 91.

The problems that pupils complain most about in science are numerical problems in chemistry and physics (particularly mechanics and electronics), including the manipulation of formulae, and certain types of problem-solving in biology. Many students are unsure about how to develop a science assignment and they have only vague pictures in the mind of scientific principles.

Certain areas seem to engender total bewilderment. 'What is going on here?' asked Claire about a genetics problem. 'I don't understand.' When I probe I find that: she does not (i) understand the terms 'dominant' and 'recessive'; (ii) she is uncertain about reduction division (meiosis) when the sex cells are formed; and (iii) the symbols confuse her. The problem is about crossing and in it R causes red colour and r is albino:

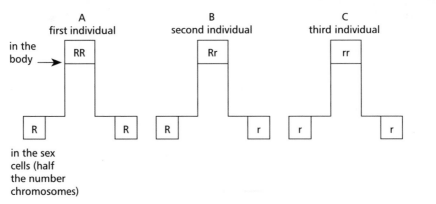

When fertilization occurs between A and B:

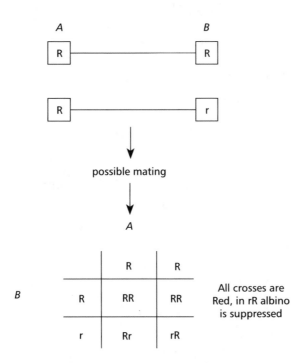

possible mating

	R	R
R	RR	RR
r	Rr	rR

All crosses are Red, in rR albino is suppressed

When B is mated with C:

C

	r	r
R	Rr	Rr
r	rr	rr

B

Equal numbers
(Rr) and
albino (rr)

A with C:

A

	R	R
r	Rr	Rr
r	Rr	Rr

C

all offspring
(babies) are
Red because in Rr

If B individuals mate with each other:

B

	R	r
R	RR	Rr
r	rR	rr

B

3 red,
1 Albino
(rR = Rr)

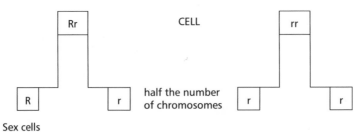

Rr   CELL   rr

R   r   half the number
of chromosomes   r   r

Sex cells
(eggs, sperms)

The above illustrates why so many pupils find science difficult. A seemingly simple problem involving *one* dominant and *one* recessive factor can include several concepts. You need to have *clear*, separate images in your mind of each of these processes or concepts – the understanding of the whole depends on the clear understanding of each individual component. The overall picture is fuzzy otherwise. What is needed is *concept building*, that is, taking each abstract idea, translating them separately into *concrete* terms and then knitting together the ideas into a whole. First come the general ideas, like fertilization, then more specific ideas like dominant and recessive and, finally, use of symbols to represent some of these ideas:

This is time-consuming but there can be *no short cut* for total comprehension. One great difficulty, even with the diagrams shown, is that circles with letters in are essentially abstract, even though they represent real things and real events. To link more effectively with real life you could imagine Rr as a red frog with a cell magnified showing an imaginary couple of genes, one dominant (R) and large, the other recessive (r) and tiny. (The words 'large'/'tiny' convey some of the meaning.) Drawings are even more effective. The image created in the mind must be of R totally suppressing r in a pairing (see overleaf).

The aim of good learning is to create the clearest images in the mind as possible. Where something is abstract it should be translated into a concrete image, so that linkage with real-life experience in the mind is made easier. Some abstract processes (for example, the manipulation

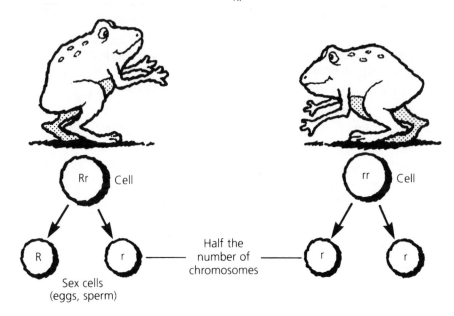

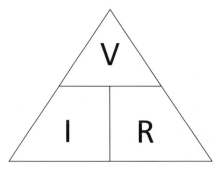

of formulae) can be linked to the already established knowledge of processes in memory. Even in this area certain mnemonics are still useful:

The triangle is an extremely useful mnemonic in electricity. It allows a student to be able to transpose easily:

$$I = \frac{V}{R} \text{ to } V = I \times R \text{ to } R \longrightarrow \frac{V}{I}$$

This does not contribute to understanding in the deep sense. It is a manipulative device, but:

$$I = \frac{V}{R}$$

means that if you increase the voltage (V), the current (I) increases if the resistance (R) is kept constant. A more *concrete* example using numbers will illustrate this:

1 = 2 amps		I = ? amps
V = 6 volts	*increase*	V = 12 volts
R = 3 ohms	to	R = 3 ohms
		$I = \frac{12}{3} = 4$ amps

So, double the voltage, double the current. Creating images in this way, building concept on concept, linking concept to concept, is of paramount importance for complete understanding. Experimental work is useful, but simply doing practical work, however well graded and organized, does not mean that understanding will be 100 per cent or that memorizing will be effective. In practical work there are many distractions for the formation of the image. For the mind, for example, resistance is an abstract concept and bears little relation to the real-life rheostat (variable resistance) being used. Ultimately, diagramming and the careful separation of concepts (ideas) is the answer to good learning in science.

LABORATORY WORK

Students frequently remember the *experience* of working in the laboratory, but they forget the process or principle.

'Oh, yes,' said Gail, 'I remember adding some liquid to a white powder in a test-tube. It bubbled up and shot all over my jumper.' Obviously there were screams all round and the *incident* in general was highly memorable, but the process was lost. The powder was calcium carbonate, the liquid was dilute acid:

CARBONATE + ACID ⟶ SALT + CARBON DIOXIDE + WATER

$CaCo_3 + HCl \longrightarrow CO_2 + H_2O + CaCl_2$

This can be usefully mnemonicized in story form as:

On the **car bonnet** (*carbonate*) it **acid**-rained giving **sea-o-too** (CO_2 – Carbon Dioxide) + **water**.

The mnemonic is imperfect because the second part does not link directly to the reality of the process ('sea-o-too' is a play on sounds, whereas a car bonnet having acid-rain falling on it closely approximates to the process involved).

Two other processes can be linked to the above:

1 ACID + METAL ⟶ SALT + HYDROGEN (H_2)
2 ACID + BASE ⟶ SALT + WATER (H_2O)

Translated to image form:

1 As Sid **Met** Al he was led to an old **Salt** and '**H**' too (H_2).
2 A met B and made **Salt-Water** (a seaman – AB).

As *salt* is in all three, the above can be filed:

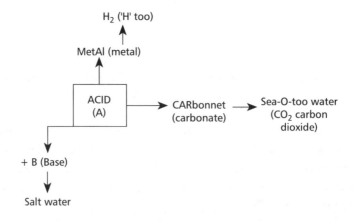

The links between the word-mnemonics are of vital importance, so each *process* needs to be learnt as a story; the shorter and more vivid the story the more memorable and effective.

You may find that your own mnemonic (or your teacher's) works better for you than one in this book. In your own memory you have experiences which are totally unique and you need to link to those personal experiences. Also, a down-to-earth mnemonic is very often more effective than one that on the surface looks cleverer. In fact, silly, almost childish, mnemonics are often remembered better, especially where there is rhyme, rather like that in nursery rhymes:

As Sid Met Al
He got H too
With Car Bonnet
T'was Sea-O-too

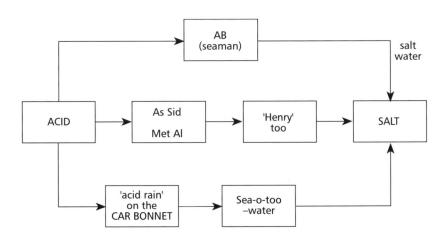

This can be filed away under 'acid reactions'. However, if it is not referred to for some time, like an unused railway line, it will be difficult to retrieve because searches for 'matches' occur more often in much *used* areas of memory. This is how 'circular thinking' develops (thinking within like or similar patterns) and you need to *learn* how to break away from such rigid patterns by *lateral thinking*, as described earlier in

Chapter 2, by opening up unused memory areas and linking unrelated items from memory.

LEARNING THROUGH PROBLEM-SOLVING

The above illustrates how the careful organizing of science work can produce highly memorable images and also result in deep understanding. However, examination questions nowadays are probing pupils' skills and strategies in problem-solving as well and this demands that you are able to dissect problems successfully to determine what they *mean*. You should then be able to reassemble the elements to give one answer (convergent problems) or several answers (divergent problems).

Although practice will help you to probe the examiner's thinking and style, occasionally there is going to be a question set in an entirely different way. This will require you to approach the same work from a completely different direction. The pattern you have in your mind attached to that particular piece of work may have to be dispensed with as you search for the *new* pattern.

The important thing about practice with problems is that not only does it help you to revise facts, principles and processes, it also helps you to learn *patterns* in problems and strategies of approach.

Some typical problems

Chemistry
The electrolysis of molten sodium chloride is used in industry to make sodium and chlorine.

i   Complete the ionic equations for the reactions at the electrodes.

    Cathode $Na^+ \longrightarrow Na$
    Anode $Cl^- \longrightarrow Cl_2$

ii Which of the two electrodes (anode or cathode) is an oxidation? Explain how you know.

iii Suggest two reasons why sodium is expensive to make by this method.

Answer and explanation:

i Cathode $Na^+ + e \longrightarrow Na$
Anode $2Cl^- \longrightarrow Cl_2 + 2e$

The above is a simple gain/loss of electrons which is the basis of the formation of *ions*.

ii The mnemonic OIL RIG will tell you that *Oxidation* is *Loss* of electrons, *Reduction* is *Gain* of electrons. So, $2Cl^- \longrightarrow Cl_2 + 2e$ is oxidation.

iii Reasons for the expense of the operation (divergent thinking):

a need to keep a very high temperature to melt sodium chloride
b a current has to be passed through the molten compound for *some time* (formation of sodium is slow).

Physics

Sound travels at a depth of 1.5m in 1 millisecond (ms) in water. A boat sounds an echo and it is heard 10 milliseconds later. What is the depth of the water?

d

For the sound to travel distance d, it takes 5 milliseconds (i.e. 10 ÷ 2, down to the bottom and back up).

Therefore, the depth is 5 × 1.5m = 7.5m

Science assignments

Course-work in science is a practical experiment, or series of experiments, that you perform in the laboratory and then write-up about that practical work. The actual experimental time can be completed

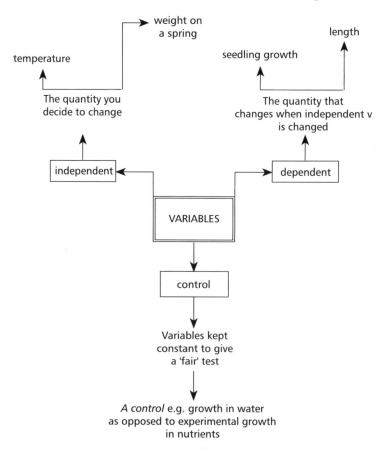

within a single hour's lesson or it may take longer. Usually, your teacher will provide you with a sheet of pointers to give some guide.

Some terms used in investigations are best explained at this point – see mind-map on previous page.

Three *skills* will be tested:

1 The *designing* of the investigation. The *variables* have to be identified.
2 *Carrying out investigations*. This means the results section. Measurements must be accurate.
3 *Interpreting* is 'searching for patterns'. To have access to GCSE Level 9 and above the *flaws* in the experiment (the uncertainty of the evidence) must be considered. You must mention other variables that are *assumed* to be constant but are impossible to control completely.

For your assignment you need an experiment in which you can alter the independent variable and measure the dependent variable; for example, measure the effect of temperature on the growth of rhizopus (a fungus). The results can be set down in the form of a table and a graph drawn. You will need to:

1 Formulate a hypothesis – 'If I perform this experiment, I expect this to happen.' You can give reasons why you expect those things to happen. For good marks it is necessary for you to fulfil your prediction.
2 Explain carefully the design and layout of your experiment. Include an explanation of what your *control* is.
3 Record your results (tables and graphs).
4 Comment fully on the results you have obtained. Detail any *improvements* you could make.
5 You will have changed *one* of the independent variables (e.g. temperature). Now, investigate the effect of changing a *second* independent variable (e.g. the concentration of nutrient solution in which a plant grows). This will allow the assignment to be marked up to Level 10.

Use of formulae to emphasize principles would make the assignment much sounder.

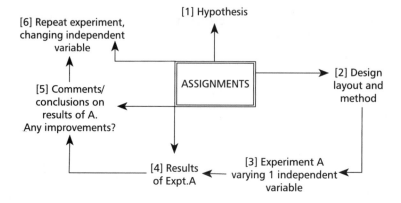

Assignment examples

1 Gary has just completed a physics assignment in which the teacher gave pointers to a cut-out paper helicopter. When paper clips are attached to the bottom, the 'wings' rotate when the structure is dropped.

Keeping the height of release constant, the number of paper clips attached is varied and the time of each drop measured. The hypothesis was that, with increased weight, the helicopter would descend faster but that as the helicopter descended faster it would also *rotate* faster and air resistance to descent would increase. The graph would there-fore not be a straight line but a curve. The results show this.

The *extension* to this experiment is to repeat it and vary the wing size, keeping the number of paper clips constant. This is a simple mathematical treatment using:

Force = mass × acceleration
F = m g
Let mass of a paper clip = m

mass of paper = M
1 clip
Downward force = (m + M)g
Upward thrust = R_1 (air resistance)
Resultant downward force (F_1) = (m + M)g − R_1
2 clips
$F_2 = (2m + M)g − R_2$
Up to n clips (Gary used 8)
In the above $R_1 < R_2 < R_3 \ldots \ldots < R_n$
$F_1 < F_2 < F_3 \ldots \ldots < F_n$

The mathematical treatment is nice for the teacher to receive, but careful wording can achieve the same objective.

2 Ravi investigated the reaction between nitric acid and marble chips. The variables identified were:

a the concentration of acid
b volume of acid
c type of acid
d temperature of acid
e mass of limestone
f surface area of chips
g time of contact

The *planning section* discussed the following:

1 Hypothesis about the temperature being varied.
2 Hypothesis about the concentration being varied.
3 Theoretical reasons set down for 1 and 2 (kinetic theory treatment – number of molecules taking part in collisions considered).
4 Consideration of control variables – includes b, c, e, f, g above.

There is then a diagram and chemical equation. The *Results* section includes a *table* and graphs and then a full analysis of these results.

SCIENCE: THE CORE SYLLABUS

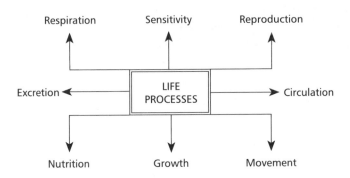

Science mind-map: theme 1

To illustrate how scientific information can be mnemonicized, the eight processes of life have been turned into story form by trying to find as many concrete *nouns* as possible that correspond closely to the eight points. Concrete nouns create clear mental images and, therefore, will more easily link to real-life experience in memory. Certain adjectives and verbs (the active ones) also produce good mental images with little mental effort:

> A *Sensitive* ant happily *Reproducing* in a flat in Chelsea was taken out of *Circulation* and chained up in a cell to restrict his *Movement*. Alas, his cell was tiny, preventing his *Growth*, he was given no *Nutrition*, even had to slop out his own *Excrement* and eventually died of a *Respiratory* disease, poor thing!

In the story the ant is the *peg* (which means that life processes can be accessed by remembering the story about 'that ant') and each of the words chosen approximates as closely as possible to the corresponding life process. Also, since each of the processes fit to corners and sides of the mind map we *must* remember that there are eight of them. This illustrates another point. It is that each file image should be as complete as possible. If you try to fit one part of the jigsaw puzzle elsewhere it may not be learnt so well. Many questions are set *within* theme areas and therefore the easily accessible files of themes are an invaluable tool for recall.

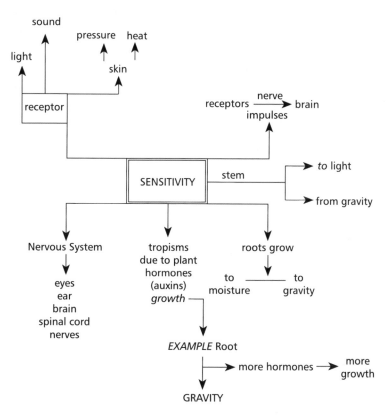

Life process (sensitivity) mind-map

This is a *map* of the theme area. The key words and processes connected with *sensitivity* are included within a small area ready for 'filing'. The layout of the map is of crucial importance for learning. Where branching results in a 'list' effect (as in the above map) there is a link with an area of memory which is in constant use (lists are an integral part of daily life).

Some key words and lists create clear mental images (pictures) and in these areas understanding is easily achieved. Other words (e.g. tropisms, auxins) need explanatory diagrams and pictures. Such words also need to be *pegged* for recall. The words 'plant hormones' are easily recalled, but the link with *auxins* is difficult to make, as is the further one to tropisms. *Auxin* is a word that looks and sounds like auxiliary and the auxins can be visualized as auxiliary fire engines produced by root and stem tips and racing down one side or other of roots and stems, *elongating* these areas and causing bending. These effects are *tropisms*, much in evidence in *tropical* rain forests where *growth* seems to have gone haywire. So: *auxiliary fire engines in the **tropics** give bags of growth **hormones**.*

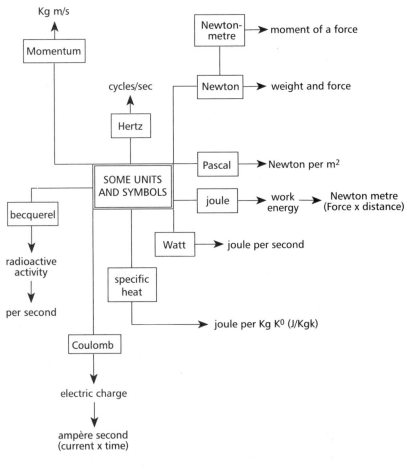

Science mind-map 1

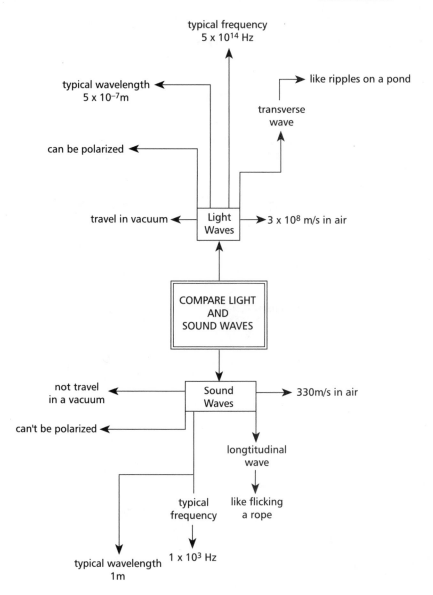

Science mind-map 2

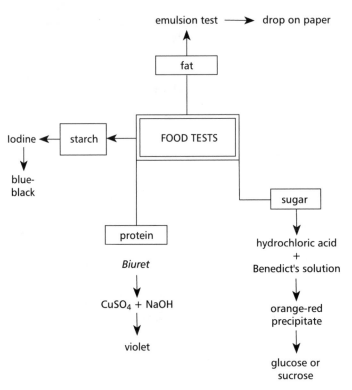

Science mind-map 3

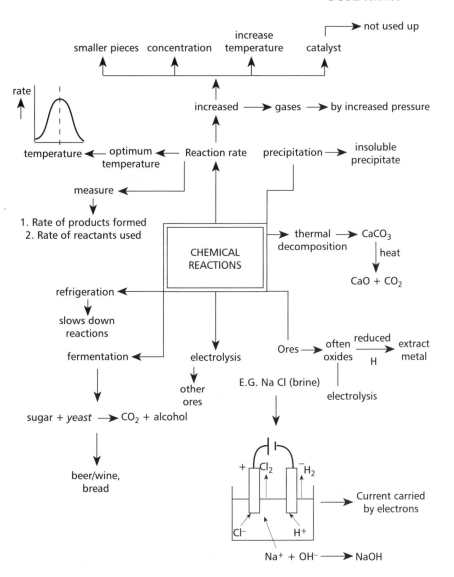

Science mind-map 4

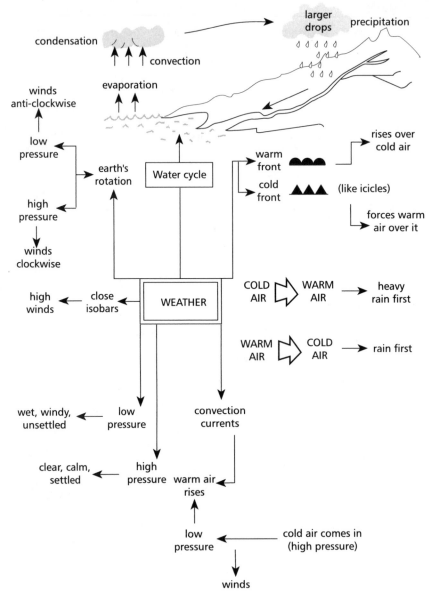

Science mind-map 5

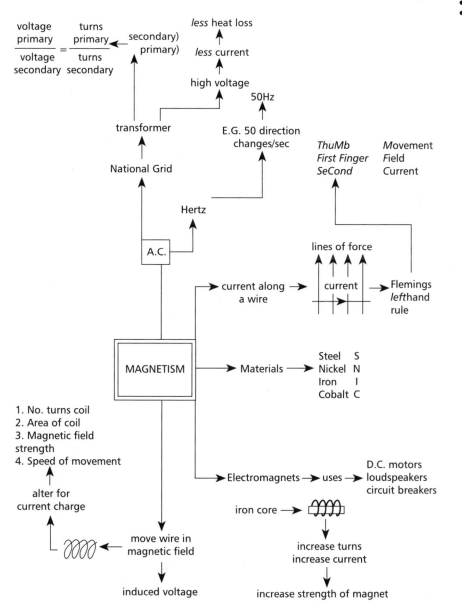

Science mind-map 6

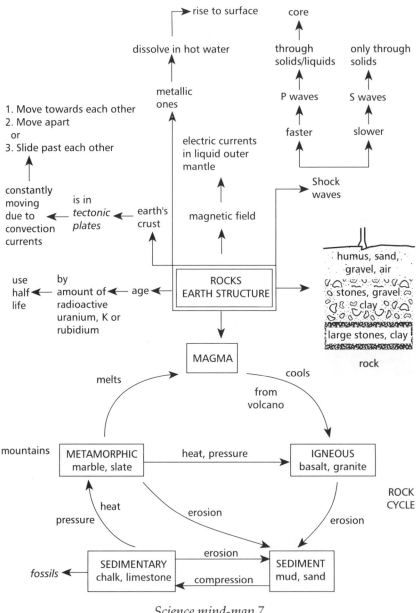

1. Move towards each other
2. Move apart
   or
3. Slide past each other

rise to surface

core

dissolve in hot water

through solids/liquids   only through solids

metallic ones

P waves   S waves

electric currents in liquid outer mantle

faster   slower

constantly moving due to convection currents

is in *tectonic plates* ← earth's crust

magnetic field

Shock waves

use half life ← amount of ← age ← radioactive uranium, K or rubidium

ROCKS EARTH STRUCTURE

humus, sand, gravel, air

stones, gravel

clay

large stones, clay

rock

MAGMA

melts   cools

from volcano

mountains

METAMORPHIC marble, slate   heat, pressure   IGNEOUS basalt, granite

ROCK CYCLE

heat pressure   erosion   erosion

SEDIMENTARY chalk, limestone   erosion   SEDIMENT mud, sand

fossils ←   compression

Science mind-map 7

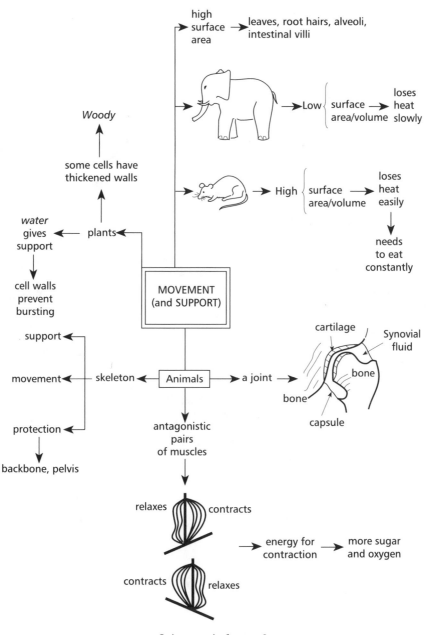

Science mind-map 8

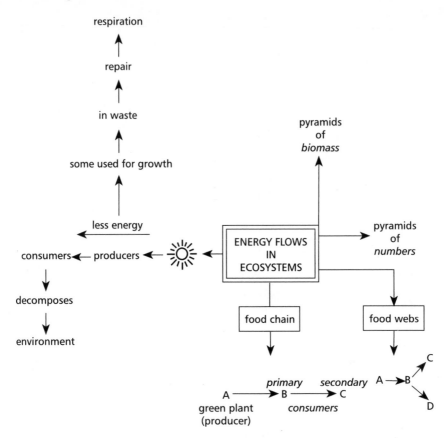

Science mind-map 9

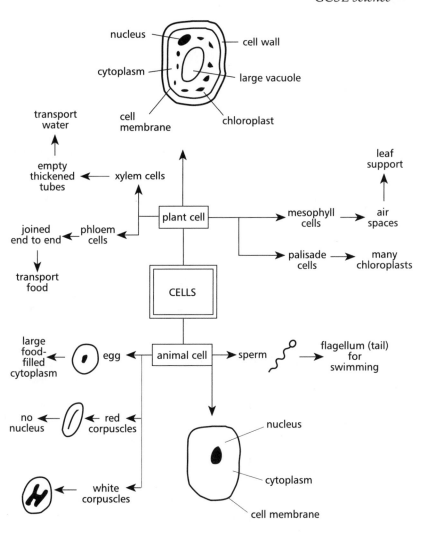

Science mind-map 10

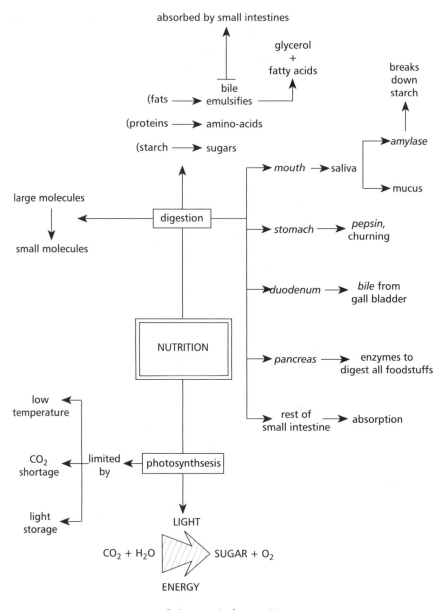

Science mind-map 11

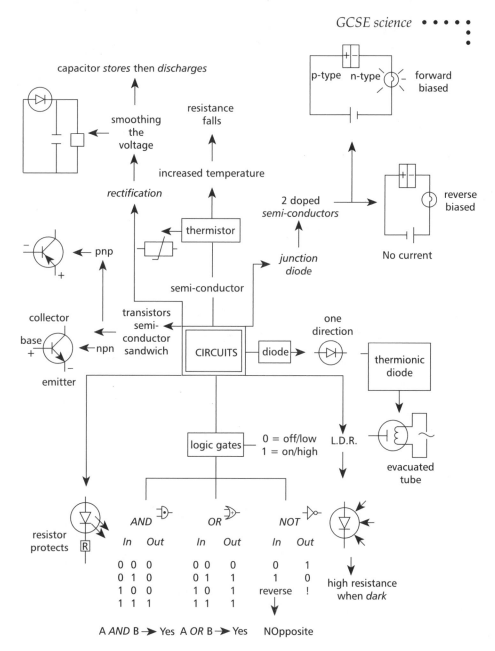

Science mind-map 12

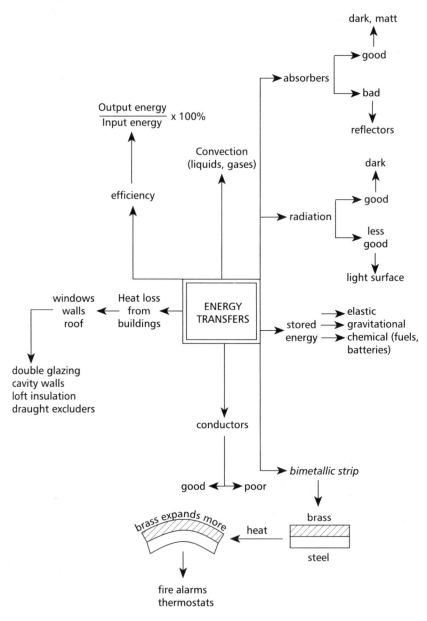

Science mind-map 13

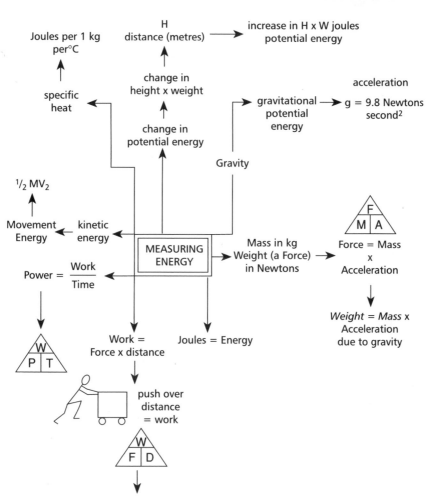

Joules per 1 kg
per°C

H
distance (metres) → increase in H x W joules
potential energy

specific
heat

change in
height x weight

change in
potential energy

gravitational → g = 9.8 Newtons
potential   second²
energy

acceleration

Gravity

½ MV₂

Movement ← kinetic
Energy   energy

MEASURING
ENERGY

Mass in kg
Weight (a Force) →
in Newtons

F
M   A

Force = Mass
x
Acceleration

Power = Work / Time

W
P   T

Work =
Force x distance

Joules = Energy

Weight = *Mass* x
Acceleration
due to gravity

push over
distance
= work

W
F   D

Force = Newtons, *distance* = metres

NOTE: Most formulae are *given* on the exam papers

Science mind-map 14

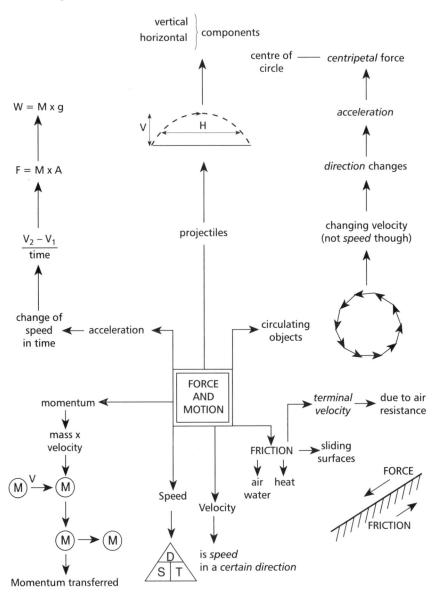

Science mind-map 15

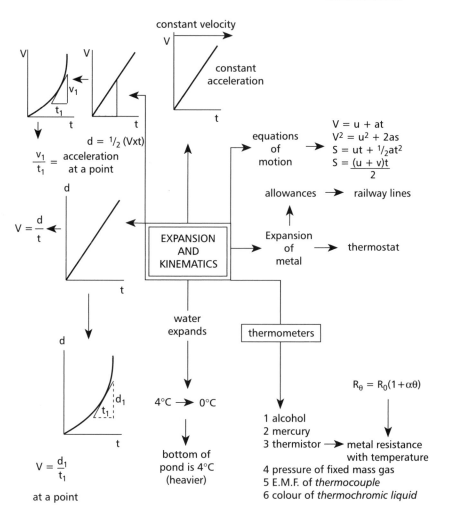

Science mind-map 16

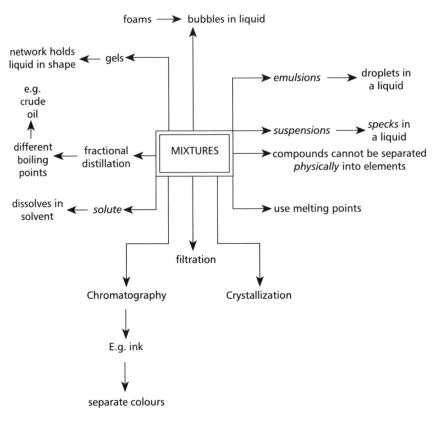

Science mind-map 17

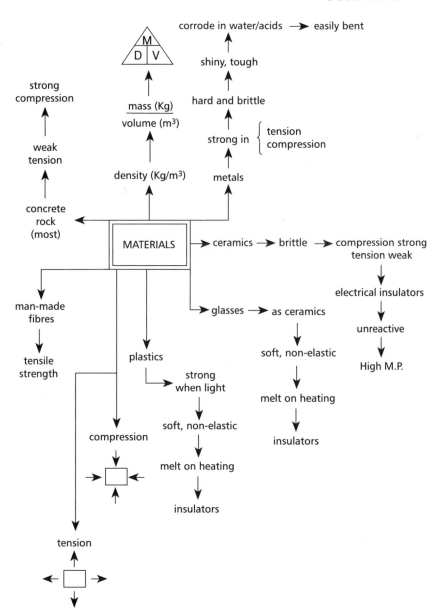

Science mind-map 18

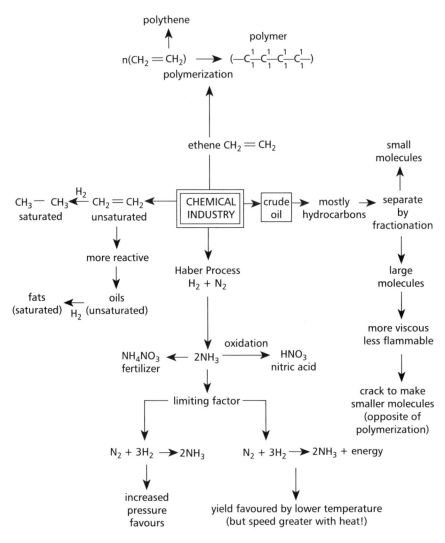

Science mind-map 19

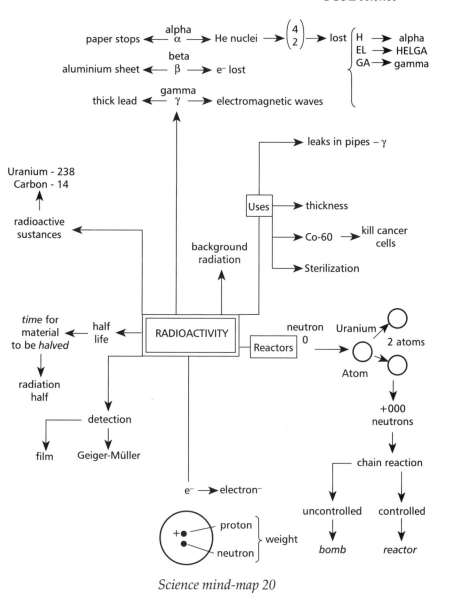

Science mind-map 20

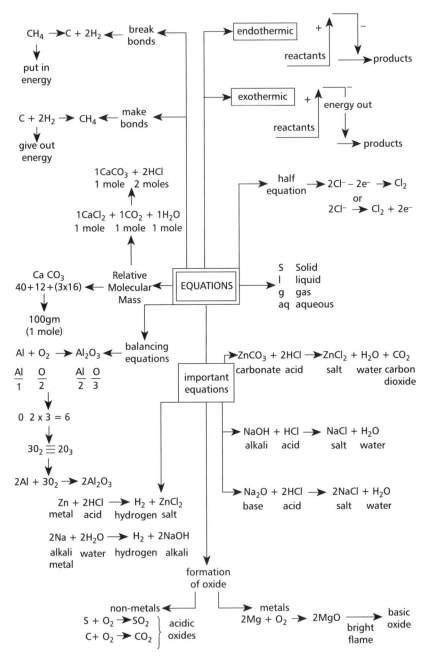

Science mind-map 21

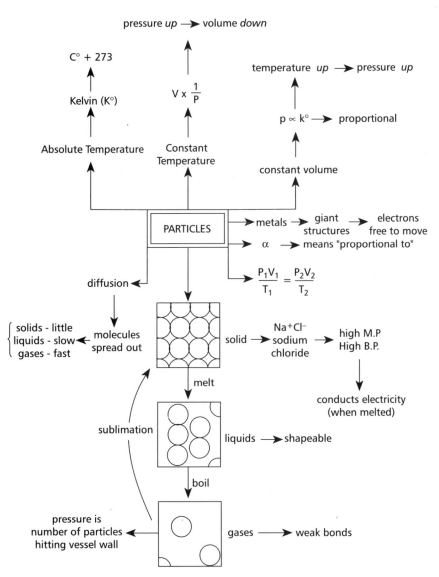

pressure *up* → volume *down*

C° + 273

Kelvin (K°)

V x $\frac{1}{P}$

temperature *up* → pressure *up*

p ∝ k° → proportional

Absolute Temperature

Constant Temperature

constant volume

PARTICLES

metals → giant structures → electrons free to move

α → means "proportional to"

$\frac{P_1V_1}{T_1} = \frac{P_2V_2}{T_2}$

diffusion

solids - little
liquids - slow
gases - fast

molecules spread out

solid → Na⁺Cl⁻ sodium chloride → high M.P High B.P.

conducts electricity (when melted)

melt

sublimation

liquids → shapeable

boil

pressure is number of particles hitting vessel wall

gases → weak bonds

Science mind-map 22

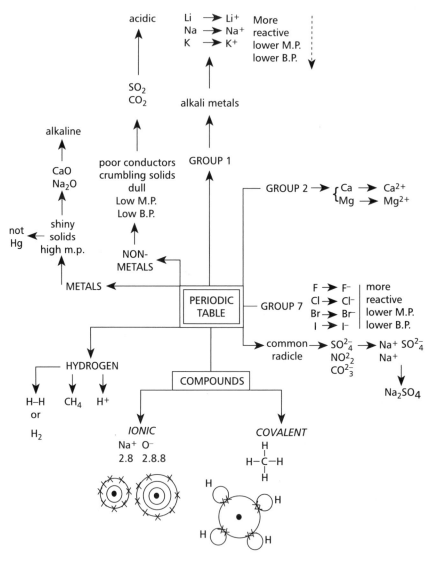

Science mind-map 23

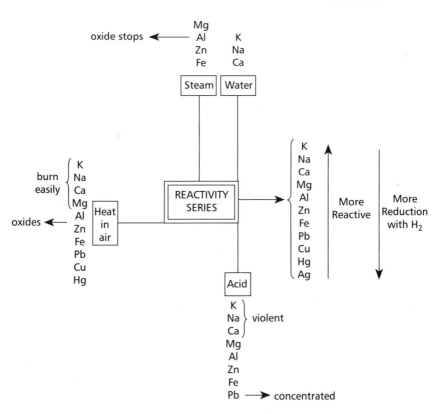

Science mind-map 24

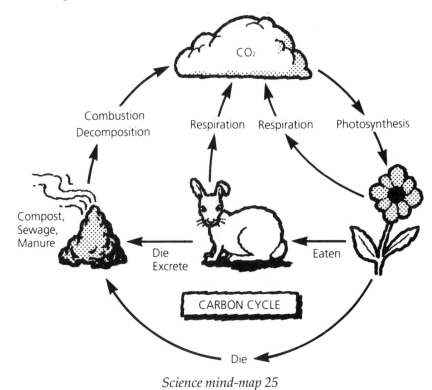

Science mind-map 25

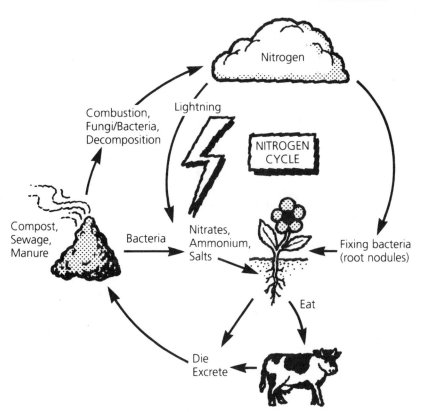

Science mind-map 26

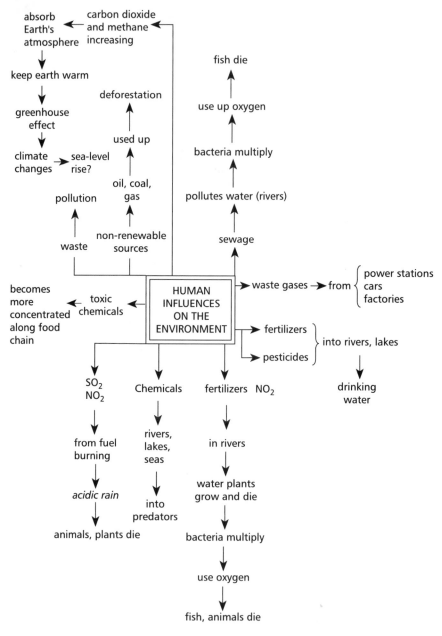

Science mind-map 27

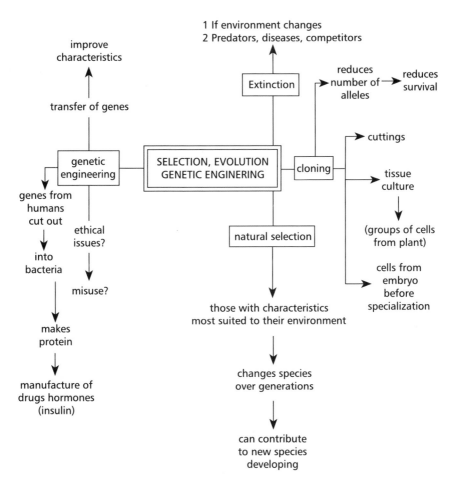

Science mind-map 28

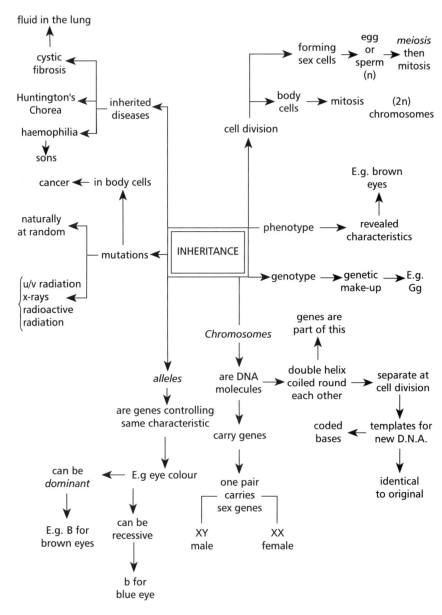

Science mind-map 29

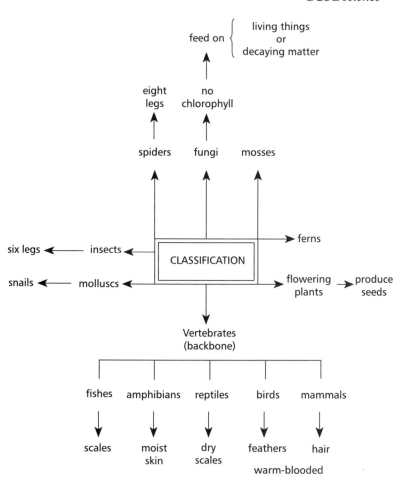

Science mind-map 30

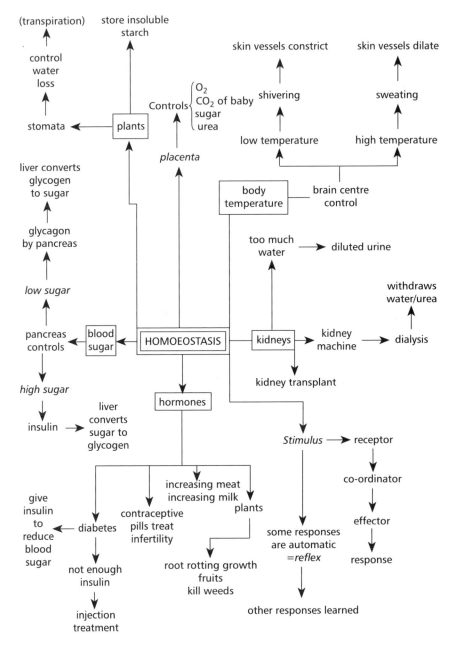

Science mind-map 31

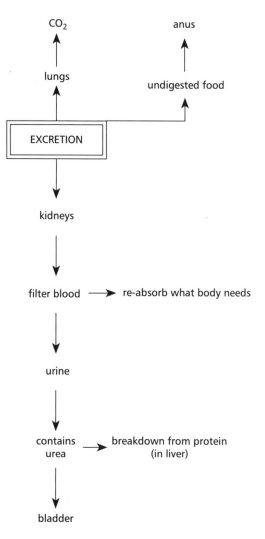

CO

Science mind-map 32

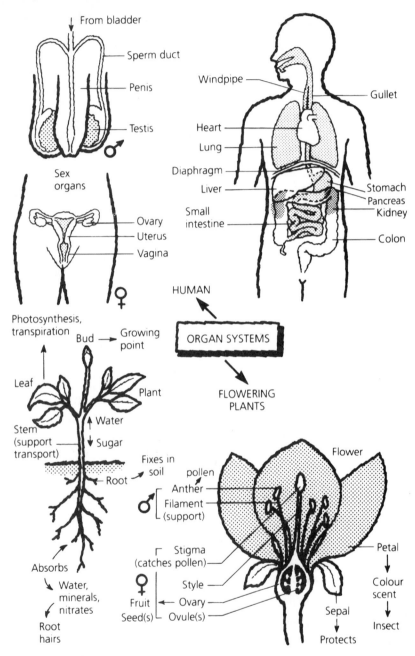

Science mind-map 33

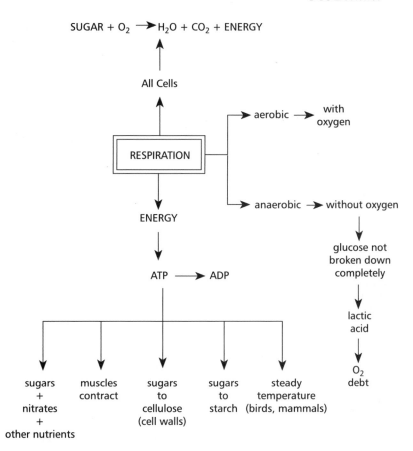

SUGAR + O_2 → H_2O + CO_2 + ENERGY

All Cells

RESPIRATION

aerobic → with oxygen

anaerobic → without oxygen

glucose not broken down completely

ENERGY

ATP → ADP

lactic acid

O_2 debt

sugars + nitrates + other nutrients

muscles contract

sugars to cellulose (cell walls)

sugars to starch

steady temperature (birds, mammals)

Science mind-map 34

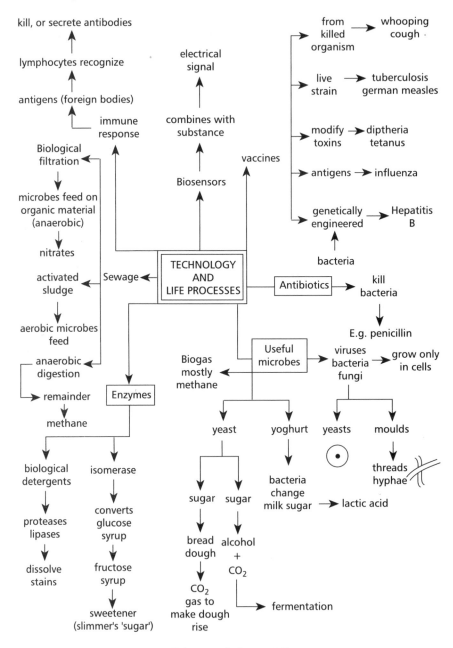

Science mind-map 35

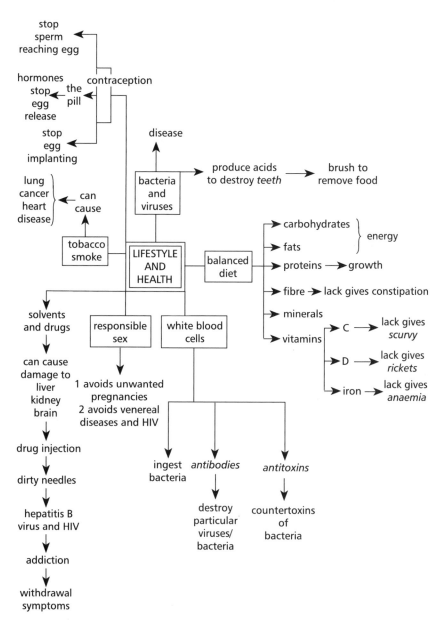

Science mind-map 36

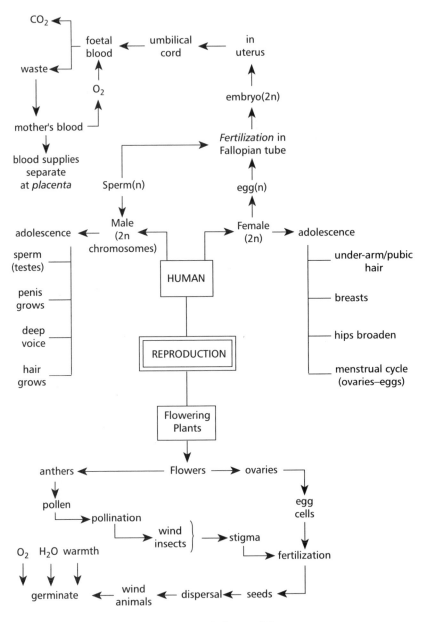

Science mind-map 37

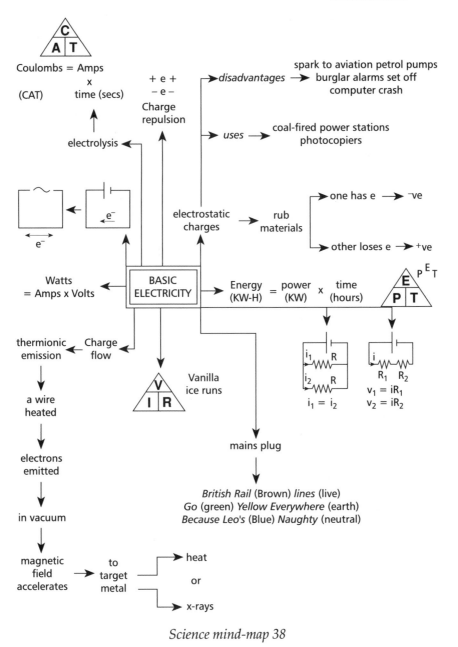

Science mind-map 38

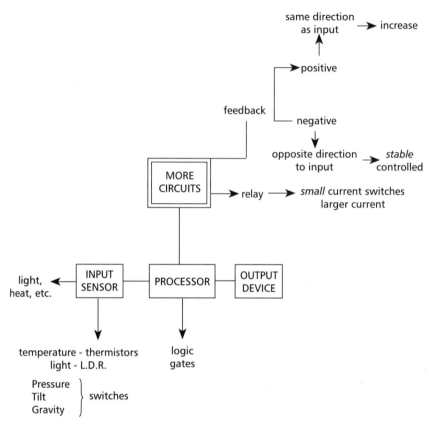

Science mind-map 39

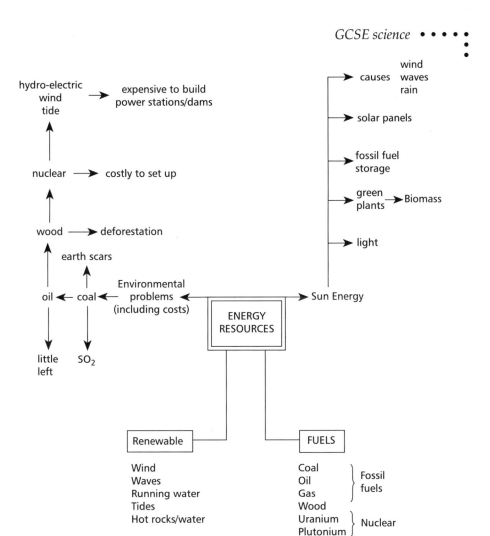

Science mind-map 40

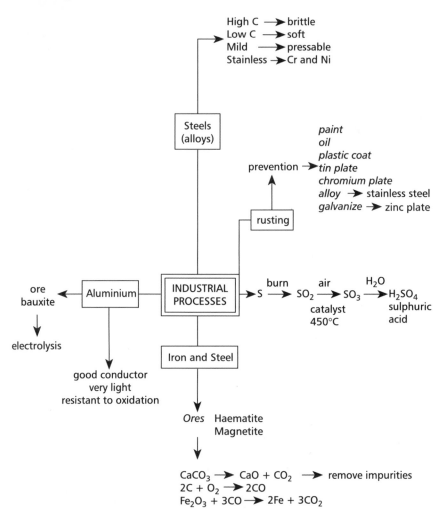

High C ⟶ brittle
Low C ⟶ soft
Mild ⟶ pressable
Stainless ⟶ Cr and Ni

Steels
(alloys)

paint
oil
plastic coat
prevention ⟶ *tin plate*
chromium plate
alloy ⟶ stainless steel
galvanize ⟶ zinc plate

rusting

ore   Aluminium   INDUSTRIAL
bauxite   PROCESSES

⟶ S ⟶ SO_2 ⟶ SO_3 ⟶ H_2SO_4
burn   air   catalyst   sulphuric
                   450°C   acid
       H_2O above SO_3

electrolysis

good conductor
very light
resistant to oxidation

Iron and Steel

Ores Haematite
Magnetite

$CaCO_3 \rightarrow CaO + CO_2 \rightarrow$ remove impurities
$2C + O_2 \rightarrow 2CO$
$Fe_2O_3 + 3CO \rightarrow 2Fe + 3CO_2$

Science mind-map 41

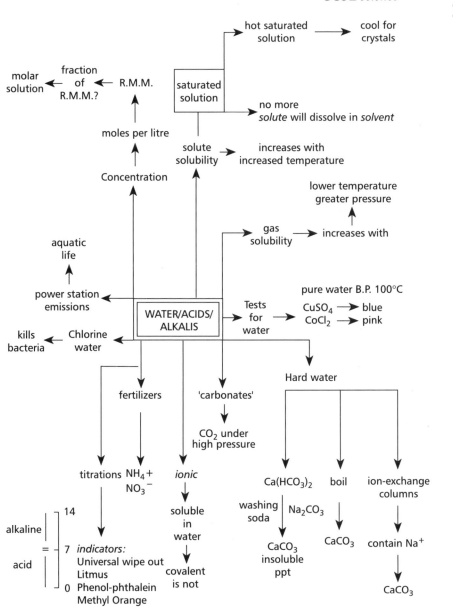

Science mind-map 42

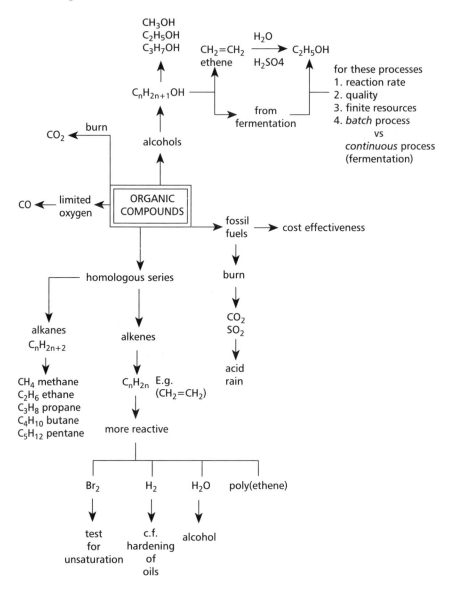

Science mind-map 43

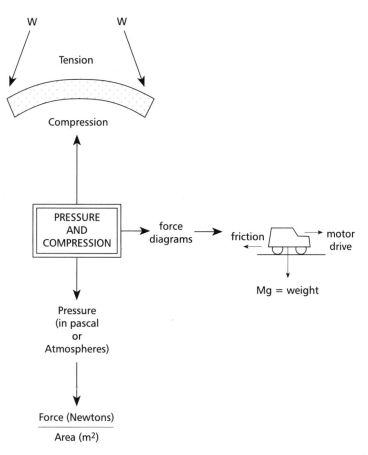

Science mind-map 44

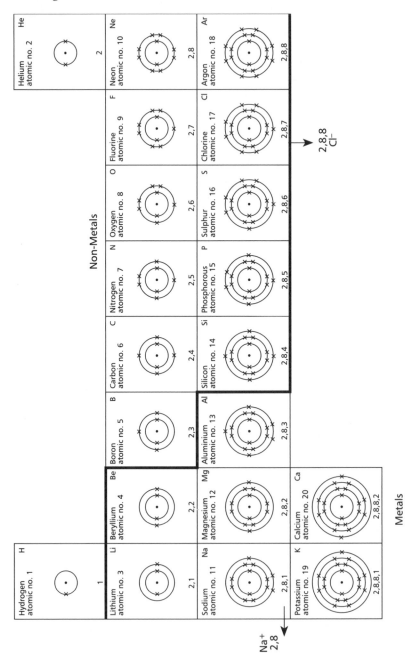

Science mind-map 45

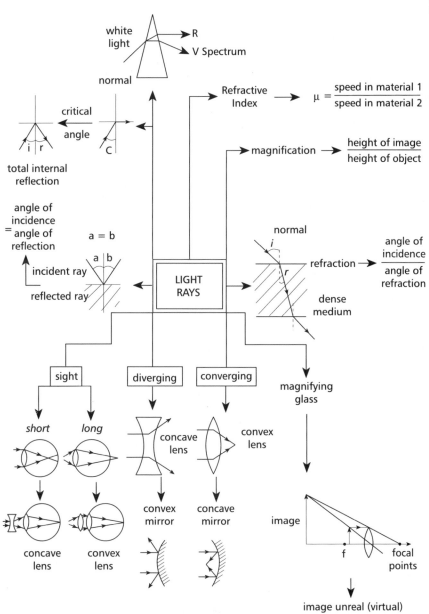

white light → R
V Spectrum

normal

critical angle

total internal reflection

i r

C

angle of incidence = angle of reflection

incident ray

reflected ray

a = b

a | b

LIGHT RAYS

Refractive Index → $\mu = \dfrac{\text{speed in material 1}}{\text{speed in material 2}}$

magnification → $\dfrac{\text{height of image}}{\text{height of object}}$

normal

i

r

refraction → $\dfrac{\text{angle of incidence}}{\text{angle of refraction}}$

dense medium

sight

diverging

converging

magnifying glass

short   *long*

concave lens

convex lens

concave lens   convex lens

convex mirror

concave mirror

image

f

focal points

image unreal (virtual)

Science mind-map 46

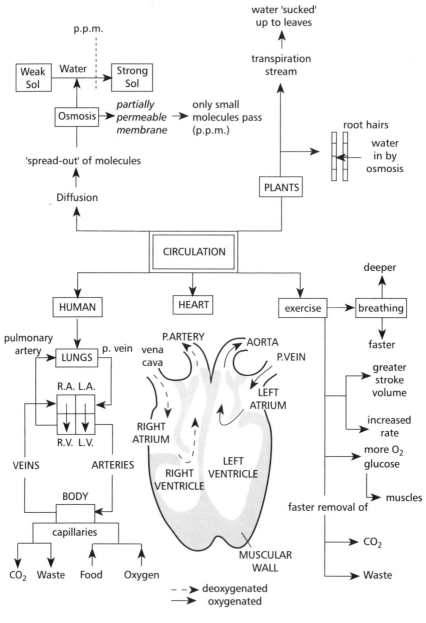

Science mind-map 47

SCIENCE: WORKED EXAMPLES

The equation for the complete combustion of butane is shown below.

$$2C_4H_{10} + 13O_2 \longrightarrow 8CO_2 + 10H_2O$$

(i) What tests could be used to prove that water and carbon dioxide are produced in the combustion reaction. For each test state the reagent used and the expected result.

Carbon dioxide

Lime Water turns 'milky

Water

Anhydrous Copper Sulphate Changes from white to blue

(ii) Calculate the mass of oxygen that would be needed to burn 116g of butane.

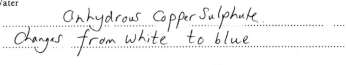

$$2C_4H_{10} = 58 \times 2 = 116$$

So, O_2 needed is $13 \times 32 =$

The mass of oxygen needed is ...... 416 g ......

(f) Complete the equation for the complete combustion of propane.

$$C_3H_8 + 5O_2 \longrightarrow 3CO_2 + 4H_2O$$

The reaction between magnesium and copper(II) sulphate solution is represented by the equation

$$Mg(s) \quad + \quad CuSO_4(aq) \quad \longrightarrow \quad MgSO_4(aq) \quad + \quad Cu(s)$$

The ion-electron equations below also represent the changes which happen in this reaction.

$$Mg \quad \longrightarrow \quad Mg^{2+} \quad + \quad 2e^-$$

$$Cu^{2+} \quad + \quad 2e^- \quad \longrightarrow \quad Cu$$

Use the equations to help you to explain why the reaction between magnesium and copper(II) sulphate solution is a **redox** reaction.

.... OIL RIG → Mg loses electrons
(Oxidation), Cu²⁺ gains electrons →
.... (reduction)

What volume of 1 mol/litre hydrochloric acid is required to react with 1 g of calcium carbonate?

(Mass of 1 mole of $CaCO_3$ = 100 g)

$$CaCO_3 \quad + \quad 2HCl \quad \longrightarrow \quad CaCl_2 \quad + \quad CO_2 \quad + \quad H_2O$$

A   10 cm³

B   20 cm³

C   50 cm³

D   100 cm³

$1g = \frac{1}{100}$ mole

$\frac{1}{100}$ mole $CaCO_3 \equiv \frac{2}{100}$ mole HCl

Volume required $= \frac{\overset{4}{\cancel{2}}}{100} \times 1000 = 20$ cm³

(B)

Figure 7 shows how the radioactivity of another isotope of technetium changes with time.

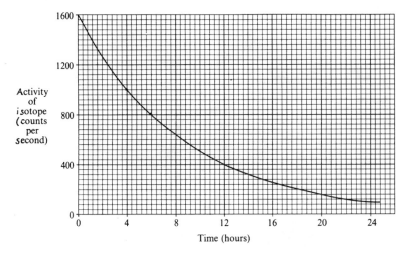

Figure 7

(i) Use the graph to work out the half-life of this isotope.

Activity, 1600 → 800 ,   time = 6 hours

In medicine, this isotope is introduced inside people's bodies.

It can show up parts which can not be seen on an X-ray photograph.

(ii) Why is it important that the isotope used inside the body has a short half-life?

Effects in the body are short-lived - esp. in formation of sex-cells.

iii) This isotope gives out gamma rays. What property of gamma rays makes this isotope suitable for this medical use?

Its penetrative property

The graph below shows the percentage yield of ammonia under differing conditions of temperature and pressure.

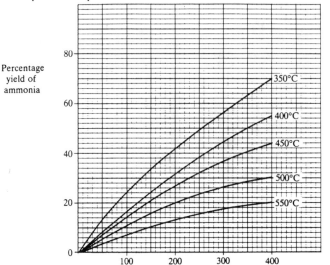

(i) Under the conditions of 200 atmospheres and 450 °C, what is the percentage yield of ammonia?

.... 42% ....

(ii) What happens to the percentage yield of ammonia if the temperature is increased at constant pressure?

.... Goes down ....

(iii) **What happens to the percentage yield of ammonia if the pressure is increased at constant temperature?**

.... Goes up ....

(iv) From your answer to (ii) suggest why a temperature of 450 °C is used.

.... It gives a reasonable yield at a ....
reasonable rate

....

Solar cells convert the light that falls on them to electrical energy. The symbol for a solar cell shown in Figure 8.

Figure 8

When light falls on the solar cell a voltage is produced across it. This voltage can be used to drive a current through a resistor placed across the solar cell.

(a) **(i)** In the space below draw a circuit diagram to show how you would connect the solar cell across a resistor so that you could measure the power being delivered to the resistor. Show the electrical meters you would need.

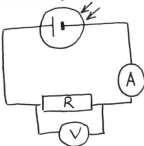

(ii) State how you would calculate the power.

Power = amps × volts

The graph below shows the current–voltage characteristics for a single solar cell of area 26 cm² and with light intensity of 15 mW/cm² falling on it.

The three straight lines represent three different resistances which could be connected to the solar cell.

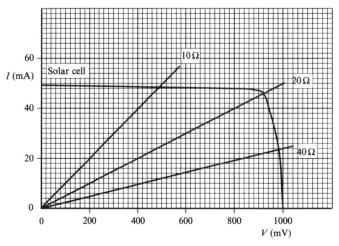

(i) Use the graph to complete the table below.

Resistance (Ω)	Voltage (mV)	Current (mA)	Power Out (mW)
10	490	48	0·49×48
20	920	46	·92×46
40	980	23·7	23.5

(ii) Calculate the power input to the solar cell.

$$15 \times 26 \ mW$$

(iii) Which resistance gives the maximum transfer of solar energy to electrical energy?

20 Ω

(iv) Calculate the efficiency of the solar cell when this resistance is connected to it.

$$\frac{0·92 \times 46}{15 \times 26} \times 100 =$$

Millions of homes in Britain now have smoke alarms. An alarm consists of two parts; a smoke detector and a horn which sounds the alarm. The diagram below represents one type of detector. It is called an ionisation detector.

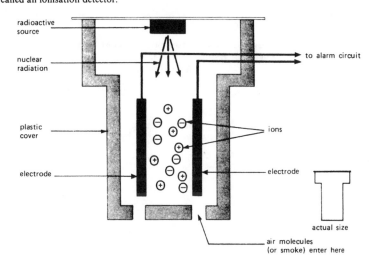

(a) When air molecules enter the detector the nuclear radiation from the source changes some of them into ions.

(i) How are ions formed?

By loss or gain of electrons

(ii) The source emits alpha radiation. Why is this source chosen?

Smoke particles impede α-rays

The ions enable an electric current to flow through the alarm circuit.

(iii) Carefully explain how the current is passed between the electrodes.

⁻ve ions attracted to one plate → release electrons. At the other plate +ve ions neutralise electrons → flow in circuit.

(continued on next page . . .)

Question continued . . .

(b) When smoke particles enter the detector they reduce the current in the detector circuit. This triggers the alarm circuit making the horn sound.

(i) The sound waves produced by the horn have a wavelength of 0.132 m and a frequency of 2500 Hz. Calculate the speed of the waves.

$$V = f \times \lambda$$
$$V = 2500 \times 0.132$$

Unit .... m/s

(ii) How long will it take the first sound wave to reach a person standing 3.3 m directly in line with the alarm?

$$T = \frac{D}{V} = \frac{3.3}{2,500 \times 0.132} \; Secs.$$

(iii) Sound waves carry energy. State **three** things that could happen to this energy when the wave hits a wall.

1. *Reflected*
2. *absorbed*
3. *transmitted through the wall*

(c)

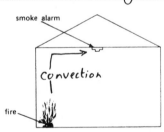

The above diagram shows the position of a smoke alarm on the ceiling of a room in which a small fire has started. Carefully explain how the smoke particles reach the smoke detector.

As the air is warmed it rises (convection) carrying smoke particles up to the alarm

Give three factors which may affect the rate at which seedlings grow.

1 *temperature*

2 *Light*

3 *moisture*

Young oat seedlings have a single straight shoot. In an investigation of the growth of oat seedlings a student marked shoots with ink at 1mm intervals.
The results are shown in the diagrams below.

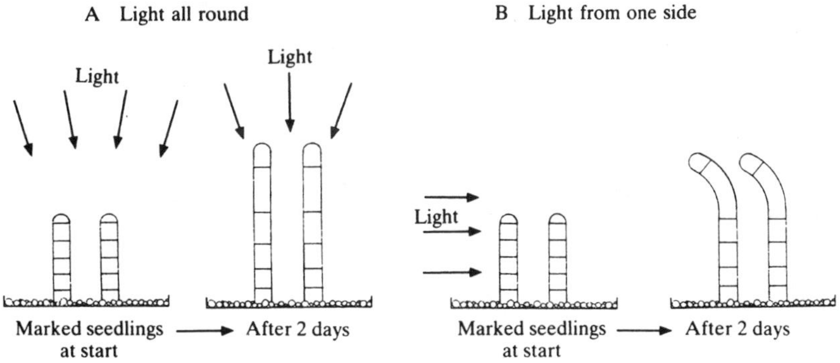

A Light all round

B Light from one side

Light

Light

Light

Marked seedlings ⟶ After 2 days
at start

Marked seedlings ⟶ After 2 days
at start

What do these results show about:-

(i) the growth of the shoot?

Shoots grow towards light

(ii) the response of the shoot to light from one side?

It turns towards the light

(i) Name the response shown by the seedlings to light from one side.

positive phototropism

(ii) Explain why this response is important to the seedlings.

Seedlings need light to grow
So it enables the maximum absorption
of light.

The student then carried out another experiment. She covered the tip of a shoot with a small piece of black paper. She shone light from one side onto the shoot.

The result is shown in the diagram below.

Black paper cap.

Seedlings at start

Light

After 2 days

Suggest a hypothesis to explain these results.

The root tip is the response area

The diagrams below show another experiment carried out by the student. She grew more seedlings and coated some on one side with substance X. The result is shown in the diagram below.

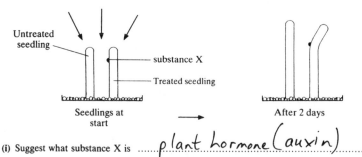

Light all around

Untreated seedling

substance X

Treated seedling

Seedlings at start

After 2 days

(i) Suggest what substance X is *plant hormone (auxin)*

(ii) Explain how this substance is involved in the response of shoots to light from one side. *Light induces increased auxin production along the side opposite to the light source*

Bleach is sodium chlorate(I) solution. It is made by mixing chlorine gas with sodium hydroxide solution. The products are sodium chloride, sodium chlorate(I) and water.

$$| \ Cl_2(g) \ + \ 2\,NaOH(aq) \ \longrightarrow \ NaCl(aq) \ + \ |\ NaClO(aq) \ + \ H_2O$$

What mass of chlorine is needed to make 14 tonnes of sodium chlorate (NaClO)?
(Relative atomic masses: Cl 35; H 1; Na 23; O 16.)

$$NaClO = 23 + 35 + 16 = 74$$

$$1 \times NaClO = 1 \times Cl_2$$
$$74 \text{ tonnes} = 2 \times 35 = 70 \text{ tonnes}.$$
$$\rightarrow 14 \text{ tonnes} = \frac{14}{74} \times 70 \text{ tonnes } Cl_2$$

The diagram below shows a loaded spring mounted vertically.

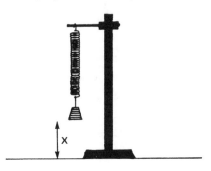

The distance from the bench to the bottom of the load is indicated by X. The distance X was measured for various loads. The results are shown in the graph below.

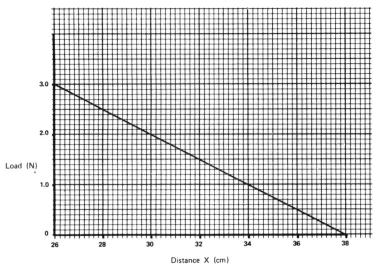

Distance X (cm)

(a) (i) Use the graph to find the value of X that corresponds to a load of 2.0 N.

$$30 \, Cm$$

(ii) What is the mass of the 2.0 N load? (Gravitational field strength = 10 N/kg.)

$$M = \frac{W}{G} = \frac{2}{10} = 0.2 \, kg.$$

continued

continued . . .

(iii) This 2.0 N load falls from the spring to the bench. Calculate the change in gravitational potential energy of the load.

Change in Gravitational Potential Energy =
Weight × Change in height (Data Book)
= 2 × 30 N cm = 60 N cm

(b) A load is attached to the unstretched spring and released. It moves up and down several times before coming to rest.

(i) Describe how the load's gravitational potential energy changes as the load moves **down**.

It loses gravitational potential energy.

(ii) Describe how the load's kinetic energy changes as the load moves **up** from its lowest position.

kinetic energy decreases to high point.

(iii) What happens to the spring's elastic potential energy as the load moves down?

"Stretching" — elastic potential energy increases.

(c) The teacher tells the pupils not to hang loads greater than 4 N from the spring. Explain why.

May stretch the spring beyond the elastic limit

(d) Give **two** uses made of the elastic properties of springs.

1. Bathroom Scales

2. Mattresses.

Turn o

A fan heater warms the room more quickly than an electric fire.

The diagram below shows the electric circuit inside a fan heater.

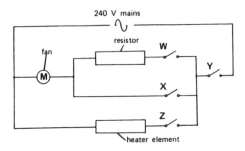

(i) Place ticks in the table below to show which switches have to be **on** to give the result shown.

RESULT	SWITCH W	SWITCH X	SWITCH Y	SWITCH Z
Slow cold air blown.	✓		✓	
Fast cold air blown.		✓	✓	
Slow hot air blown.	✓		✓	✓
Fast hot air blown.		✓	✓	✓

Resistor reduces Current → slow fan.

(ii) What could happen to the fan heater if the fan stopped when the heater element was switched on?

Overheating

(iii) Switches W and Y are linked so that they are on or off together. Suggest a reason for this.

So that the fan is not left on by mistake

The students carried out an experiment to investigate the relationship between photosynthesis and respiration.

Their investigation took place during the day on the seashore in four rock pools of similar size.

The diagrams below show the organisms each pool contained and the conditions in each pool.

Pools **1**, **3** and **4** contained the same amount of seaweed.

Pools **2** and **4** contained the same number of animals.

The pH of each pool was measured at the beginning of the investigation and after six hours.

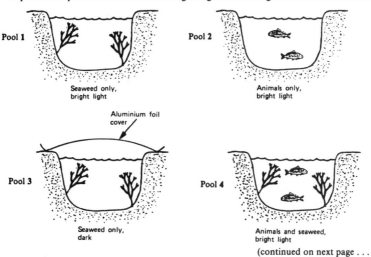

Pool 1

Seaweed only, bright light

Pool 2

Animals only, bright light

Aluminium foil cover

Pool 3

Seaweed only, dark

Pool 4

Animals and seaweed, bright light

(continued on next page . . .

Their results are shown in the table.

pH OF SEAWATER IN THE POOL	POOL			
	1	2	3	4
At the start	8.0	8.0	8.0	8.0
After 6 hours	8.5	6.5	7.2	8.0

The pH of seawater is normally 8.0

Use your knowledge of photosynthesis and respiration and the following patterns to answer the question below.

1. Carbon dioxide gas dissolves in water to form a weak acid.

2. When oxygen gas dissolves in water it has no effect on pH.

3. All living organisms respire all of the time.

Explain carefully what might have been happening in each pool to have produced the final pH measurements.

Pool 1 *Seaweed uses up CO_2 in photosynthesis → pH goes up.*

Pool 2 *CO_2 expired by fishes to reduce pH*

Pool 3 *No photosynthesis but still respiration Result as in Pool 2 → pH reduced because of CO_2 increase*

Pool 4 *Balanced environment No change in pH*

An electric wheelchair uses a 24 volt rechargeable battery. The table below gives data about the battery and the electric motor.

Technical Data

Motor : 24 V D.C. permanent magnet

Maximum speed : 5 km/h

Current drawn by motor running at maximum speed : 6 A

Time taken to discharge battery with motor running at full speed : 3.5 h

(a) Complete the sentences by adding the missing words.

When the battery is being charged _____electrical_____ energy is changed

to _____chemical_____ energy.

When the wheelchair is accelerating, energy from the battery is used to give the

wheelchair _____kinetic_____ energy.

(b) (i) What is the maximum distance that the wheelchair could travel with the motor running at maximum speed?

....

(ii) In practice the actual distance that the wheelchair will travel is less than the calculated maximum. Suggest **three** reasons why.

1. *Friction between the wheels and the roadway.*

2. *Some energy is lost in conversion of chemical → electrical energy.*

3. *Energy is lost in the motor — as heat and in conversion of electrical energy to kinetic.*

The velocity-time graph below shows a journey made by the wheelchair.

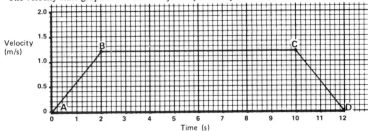

(i) Calculate the acceleration between points A and B on the graph.

$$\frac{1 \cdot 2 - 0}{2} \ m/s^2$$

(ii) Describe the motion of the wheelchair between points B and C.

Constant velocity

(iii) Calculate how far the wheelchair travelled between A and D.

Area beneath the graph =
Area of the trapezium
→ $\frac{1}{2}(BC + AD) \times 1\cdot2$
→ $0\cdot6 \times 20$ → 12 metres

(d) Calculate the power of the motor when the wheelchair is being driven at maximum speed.

$P = V \times I = 24 \times 6$ Watts
= 144 Watts

(e) The total mass of the wheelchair and the disabled person is 100 kg. Calculate the total kinetic energy of the person and the wheelchair when the wheelchair is travelling at a speed of 1.2 m/s.

$K.E. = \frac{1}{2} MV^2$
$= \frac{1}{2} \times 100 \times (1\cdot2)^2$
$= 72 \ kg \ m^2 \ s^{-2}$

GCSE maths

Maths is a subject, more than any other, in which difficult concepts are built upon simpler ones. We must learn to divide before understanding and manipulating fractions. We must have an awareness of ratio before being clear about trigonometry.

GOOD FOUNDATIONS

The need to have something in memory to which 'higher order' work can be linked, is crucial in maths. An 'all-or-nothing' rule operates and leads to loss of confidence in maths classes much more often than in other subjects. For instance, in a typical scenario David sits in a maths class trying to understand, say, some algebraic process. Try as he might he cannot visualize what is going on; yet Kubadia, sitting a few seats away, understands immediately. David was away when an earlier lesson laid the foundation for Kubadia's quick comprehension. It only takes a few of these incidents for David to begin to rate himself as being 'no good' at maths, when all he needs is re-grounding in what is known as a prerequisite (earlier building block) to the present algebra.

I had a similar experience when trying to work out transformations in wallpaper designs in a postgraduate maths class. I just could not figure out what was going on, whereas the woman in front of me could work things out in a matter of seconds (although she was not very good at the traditional maths).

'You're an absolute genius,' I said.

'It's easy,' she replied, 'after all, I've been designing patterns for quilts for years now. It's my hobby.'

At the time the significance of that remark didn't sink in. I assumed that she was probably born with some innate ability to reflect complicated patterns at will. Maybe she had inherited an exceptional ability to distinguish form; but she still needed that prerequisite practice before being able to complete mathematical transformations so well.

In algebra I often find, even with A-level students, that simple manipulations or processes are not fully understood. Just last week, someone preparing for his A-level exam (and on course for a grade A) came to a full stop in the middle of quite a difficult problem.

'How do you divide a fraction by a fraction?' he asked. (This was made a little more difficult because the fractions were algebraic ones.) In simultaneous equations, GCSE students are floored not necessarily by the overall process but by prerequisites like directed numbers $(- \times - = +)$.

Maths is also difficult because much of it is abstract, full of processes that need to be learnt but which are difficult to relate to real-life experience. Generally speaking, in areas like algebra, a body of knowledge can be built up without referring to real life. To pass the GCSE exam you do not necessarily need to refer

$$2\,x^2 + 3x - 14 = 0$$

to real life. Whole bodies of knowledge can be built up by visualizing processes which have a meaning only within the language of maths. Sometimes, however, a problem from the Higher Level paper makes the connection with real life for you:

The width of a rectangular area of a field is 4 metres less than its length. The area enclosed is 60m². What are the dimensions of the rectangle?

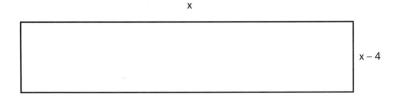

Area = (x)(x – 4) = x² – 4x = 60
So, x² – 4x – 60 = 0
  (x + 6)(x – 10) = 0
That is, x = – 6 (not possible)
    and x = 10
So, *Length = 10 metres*
Width = 6 metres

Transposing

Visualizing operations at a superficial level is useful for completing standard problems. Transposing a formula can be learnt as such an operation, without the slightest recourse to what it all means.

3x + 4 = y
move + 4 to right-hand side, change sign
3x = y – 4
divide both sides by 3
x = y – 4 completed
    3

You store the operations in your mind then apply them when you recognize something related. The recognition of the type of problem is (hopefully) linked to memory of the operations. Reawakening one, reawakens the other. However, if a problem tackles transposing from a different angle a normally competent student can flounder:

$$y = 3x + 4$$

If the dependent variable (y) is increased three times, what is the resultant change in the independent variable (x)? This needs transposing:

$$x = \frac{y-4}{3} \longrightarrow x = \frac{3y-4}{3}$$

which is the required answer.

Equations create difficulty and simply trying to *learn* operations like the above neglects the deep understanding that a 'factory system' can create (i.e. like a production line – you put in the information at one end and the finished product comes out at the other). So:

$$x \longrightarrow \boxed{\times 3} \longrightarrow \boxed{+4} \longrightarrow y$$
$$x \longleftarrow \boxed{\div 3} \longleftarrow \boxed{-4} \longleftarrow y$$

Or, $\dfrac{y-4}{3} = x$

Using numbers makes the operation more concrete:

If $x = 2$

$$2 \longrightarrow \boxed{\times 3} \longrightarrow \boxed{+4} \longrightarrow y = 10$$

$$2 \xrightarrow{\hspace{2cm} \times 3 + 4 \hspace{2cm}} 10$$

$$\div 3 \longleftarrow -4$$

This way of teaching the solving of equations makes the learning of functions and inverses for the higher level easier:

$$f(x) = 3x + 4$$
$$f(x)^{-1} = \frac{x-4}{3}$$

$$x \xrightarrow{\hspace{3cm}} f(x)$$
$$f(x)^{-1} \xleftarrow{\hspace{3cm}} x$$

REORGANIZATION

What we have seen above emphasizes several principles of maths learning. Every new aspect of maths should be built upon essential processes already in memory. For example:

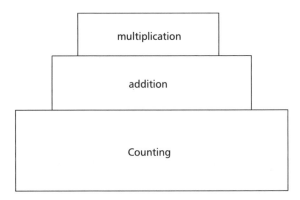

In the following mind maps, the GCSE maths syllabus is themed so that closely related processes are filed away together. However, problems will often demand that you link information from different mental files and you will need practice in problem solving of this type.

Wherever possible, problems should be worked out from basic principles and processes linked to real life. Even at A-level I try to get students to abandon rules, to work from first principles, to make diagrams and mental images. Creating *understanding* is superior to learning *rules*. You will develop confidence and become far better at maths.

Dependent probability is a case in point. Students invariably try to learn formulae when the solving of problems is easier if the *meaning* of dependent probability is clearly understood. So:

> Q In a biscuit barrel are 4 biscuits, 3 chocolate and 1 plain. Two
>   biscuits are taken at random and eaten, one after the other.
>   What is the probability that both were chocolate?

Normally, pupils draw a tree diagram:

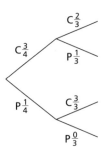

Then,

$p(A \text{ and } B) = P(A) \times p(B/A) = \frac{3}{4} \times \frac{2}{3} = \frac{1}{2}$

The process does not give a clear image in the pupils' minds.

But we could look at the problem like this:

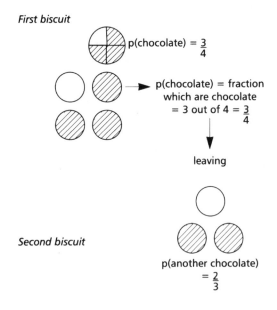

First we took $\frac{3}{4}$ ⟶   ⟶ $\frac{3}{4}$

Now we take$= \frac{2}{3}$ of this = $\frac{2}{3}$ of $\frac{3}{4}$

⟶ $\frac{2}{3} \times \frac{3}{4} = \frac{6}{12}$

$= \frac{1}{2}$

VISUALIZING

For good learning it is essential to be able to visualize an operation or principle in your mind. Transformations, in particular, need this treatment when trying to reflect or rotate a pattern; but you also learn better if you visualize algebraic operations. The clearer the mental picture, the easier it is to work out a problem or memorize a process.

Close your eyes or stare at a blank space on a wall and try to create the picture in front of you. The best students are those who are the most capable at doing this. They are also the best at recognizing patterns in problems and are efficient in dissecting convergent problems. Practice, therefore, in these elements is most effective if a conscious effort is made to visualize your mathematics; and setting down the elements of problems and sums very clearly in diagrammatic and picture form *reinforces* visualization. Practice of this *conscious* type creates deep understanding, creating a memory to which it is easy to link further knowledge. Simply practising examples, without conscious (mental picturing) application, does not build a foundation on which more advanced work can be based.

ASSIGNMENT WORK FOR COURSE-WORK/EXAMINATIONS

The Exam Boards have defined three major strands for testing: Applications; Communication; and Reasoning, Logic and Proof.

Strand 1: Applications

This includes the way in which the work is designed, and for a high level will usually involve a consideration of variables involved. For Level 7 there must be more than one line of enquiry. For Level 9 you must demonstrate the ability to co-ordinate variables (e.g. in the example below, the variables are width, height and volume). Embarking on a new area and demonstrating original thinking will result in Level 10.

Strand 2: Communication

You should lead your investigation to the point where there is effective use of symbols and algebra. There should be *precise* and *logical conclusions*.

Strand 3: Reasoning, Logic and Proof

The investigation should be chosen initially so that the general case can be demonstrated from the specific (the reverse of mind-mapping). High-level algebraic treatment and logical conclusions *almost always* lead to very high grades.

The following is an outline of course-work by Angela, assessed and marked through the N.E.A. board:

Cylinders

Angela used paper of various lengths and widths, but the same area, to roll into cylinders.

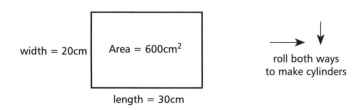

width = 20cm   Area = 600cm²

length = 30cm

roll both ways
to make cylinders

The volumes from the two cylinders were different. Angela went on to try different lengths for the same area. She found that as the radius increased and the height was reduced, the volume was greater. She used a *table* to demonstrate this.

She now produced a formula relating length with volume:

$$\text{Volume} = \frac{\text{length} \times 150}{\pi}$$

and produced two graphs:

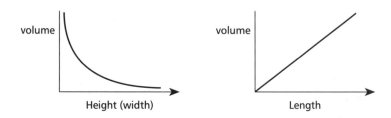

volume / Height (width)

volume / Length

(Angela could have discussed the relationship between the two graphs which would have helped to seal a top grade of 10.)

Angela discussed the meaning of the graphs separately and produced a final formula relating volume to height of the cylinder:

$$V = \frac{90000}{\pi^h}$$

The handling of algebraic formulae is very competent, although Angela could have extended the investigation by using rectangular sheets of a different area. Even so, she achieved grades of 9, 9, 9 = 27.

An assignment suggestion: How many chords?

1 Mark points on a circle. Join the points with chords:

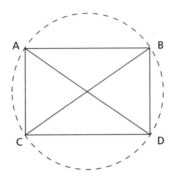

So, 4 points ⟶ 6 chords
Investigate this.

2 Make a table of these results:

Number of points	1	2	3	4	5	6
Number of chords	0	1	3	6	10	15

3 A pattern is that, however many points you have (say, 4), you have to add the numbers up to that number of points to find out how many lines there are (1 + 2 + 3 = 6).

So to find the number of lines for 20 points, you will need to add up all the numbers to 19.

This is explained by looking closer at your drawings. If there are n points, from point 1 there are $n - 1$ lines, from point 2 there are $n - 2$ lines, from point 3 there are $n - 3$ lines, and so on.

So, for 4 points there are 4 − 1 + 4 − 2 + 4 − 3 lines

$$= 6\ lines$$

4 A simpler formula is:

$$\frac{n \times (n - 1)}{2} = \text{number of chords}$$

5 Conversely, if you are presented with a sum, for example:

$$1 + 2 + 3 + 4 \ldots + 98 + 99$$

you should be able to work that out, putting n = 100, which allows you to use the above formula:

$$\frac{100 \times (99)}{2} = \text{the sum to 99}$$

Spatial thinking

For problems on symmetry, nets and 3-D trigonometry at the higher level it is essential first to construct models in 3-D. Without this prerequisite activity it is extremely difficult to visualize; a difficulty that is compounded further at A-level.

1 Card solids to be built: cube, cuboid, prism, cylinder, pyramid, tetrahedron.
2 *A Tetrahedron*

A quick way of creating a tetrahedron:

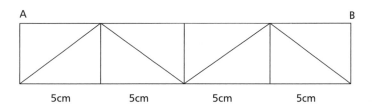

A   B

5cm   5cm   5cm   5cm

Score along vertical and horizontal lines, join the ends A to B and bend into shape:

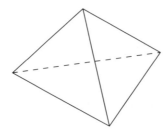

3 A cube can be further divided into 6 pyramids by joining the centre to each corner.

4 Reflection symmetry (see opposite).

5 Nets of a cube (see page 122).

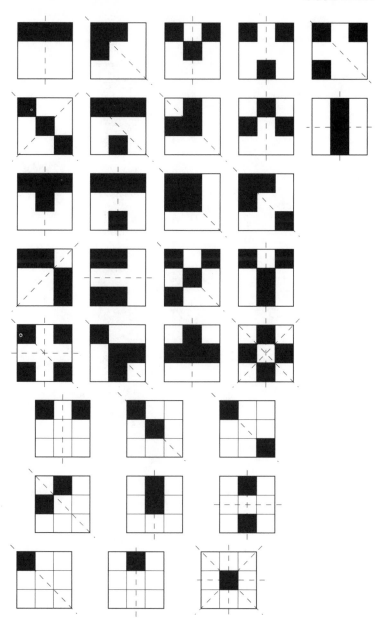

Reflection symmetry

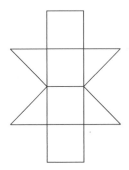

Nets of a cube

SOME GENERAL PROBLEMS

The following are some general problems to help develop thinking in maths.

1 Rotate a book through 180° once, 180° twice and end up at 90° to its original position:

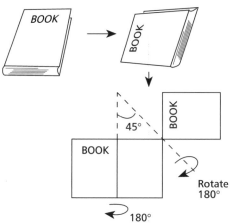

2 Find the radius:

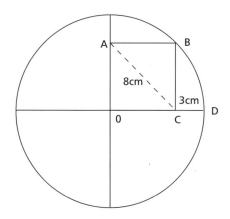

Answer

AC is 8cm and so is OB - the radius. The information leads you to try to work out the radius from CD to get OD!

3 Investigate which pairs of numbers make Pythagorean triples (3, 4, 5 for example). The set 5, 12, 13 is another (and multiples of these). There are 8 sets where all three numbers are less than 50.

MATHS: THE CORE SYLLABUS FOR A*

Maths, like science, can be visualized in mind patterns or visual forms of processes or principles. These are especially clear in the following mind-maps, which cover the Higher syllabus for maths. (The worked examples then follow on page 138.)

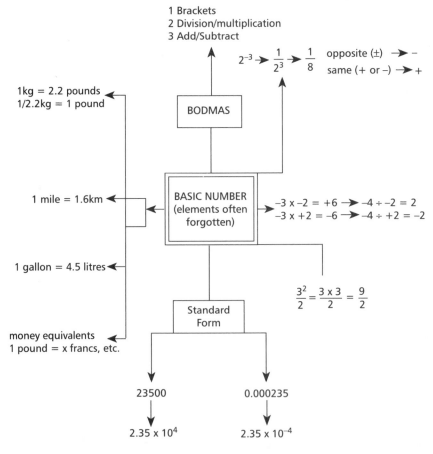

Maths mind-map 1

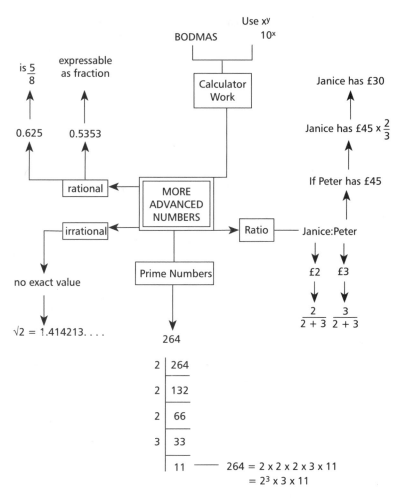

Maths mind-map 2

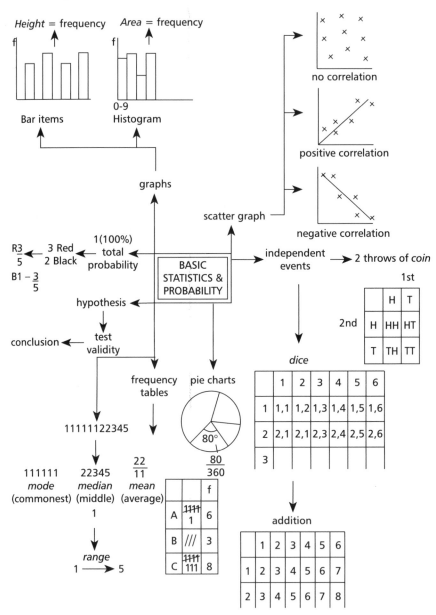

Maths mind-map 3

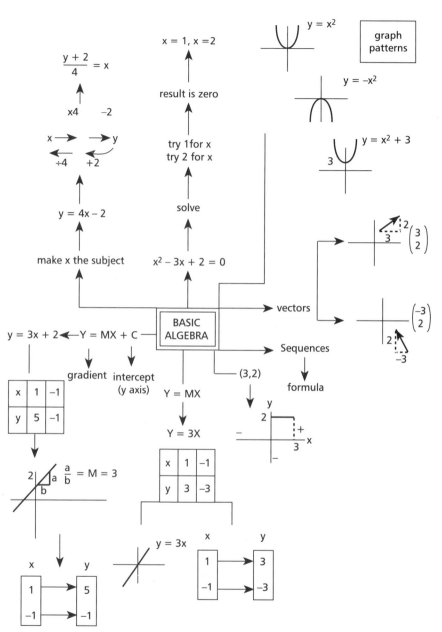

$$\frac{y + 2}{4} = x$$

↑

x4   −2

x ⟶ ⟶ y

÷4   +2

y = 4x − 2

make x the subject

x = 1, x = 2

↑

result is zero

↑

try 1 for x
try 2 for x

↑

solve

↑

x² − 3x + 2 = 0

y = x²

y = −x²

y = x² + 3

3

graph
patterns

y = 3x + 2 ← Y = MX + C ─

BASIC
ALGEBRA

⟶ vectors

Sequences

$\binom{3}{2}$

$\binom{-3}{2}$

gradient intercept
(y axis)

x	1	−1
y	5	−1

2 | a $\frac{a}{b}$ = M = 3
      b

Y = MX

↓

Y = 3X

x	1	−1
y	3	−3

(3,2)

formula

y
2
      +
─ ─ ─ ─
      3 x
−

x		y
1	→	5
−1	→	−1

y = 3x

x		y
1	→	3
−1	→	−3

Maths mind-map 4

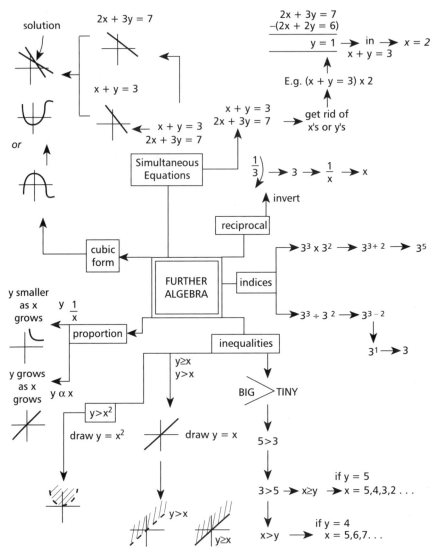

Maths mind-map 5

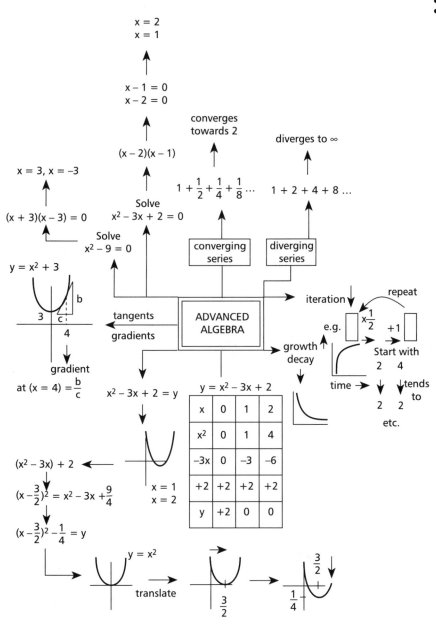

Maths mind-map 6

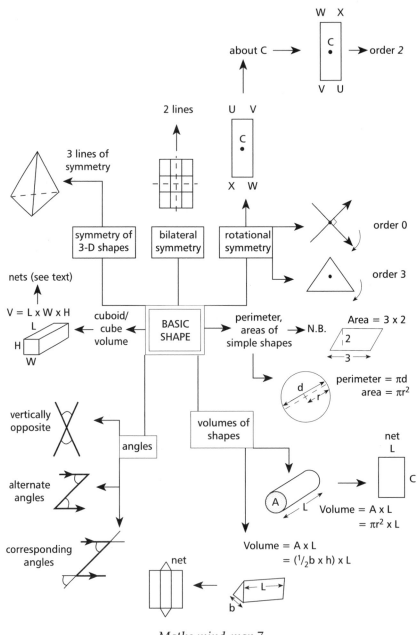

Maths mind-map 7

Symmetry

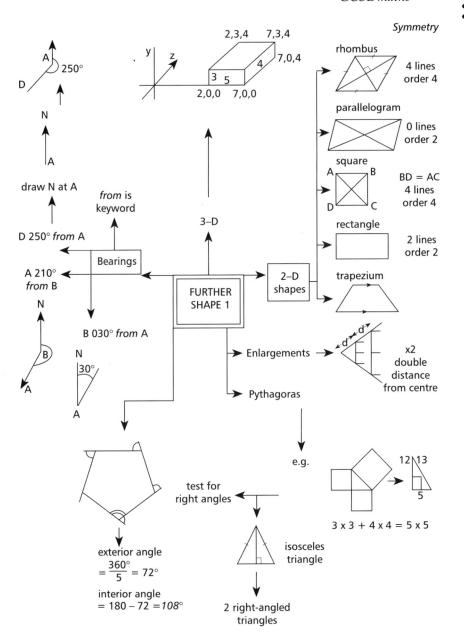

A 250°

D

N

A

draw N at A

D 250° *from* A

from is
keyword

A 210°
from B

N

B

A

B 030° *from* A

N

30°

A

3–D

Bearings

FURTHER
SHAPE 1

2–D
shapes

2,3,4   7,3,4

4   7,0,4

3 5

2,0,0   7,0,0

y   z

rhombus

4 lines
order 4

parallelogram

0 lines
order 2

square

A   B

D   C

BD = AC
4 lines
order 4

rectangle

2 lines
order 2

trapezium

Enlargements

d   d

x2
double
distance
from centre

Pythagoras

test for
right angles

isosceles
triangle

2 right-angled
triangles

e.g.

12 13

5

3 x 3 + 4 x 4 = 5 x 5

exterior angle
$= \dfrac{360°}{5} = 72°$

interior angle
$= 180 - 72 = 108°$

Maths mind-map 8

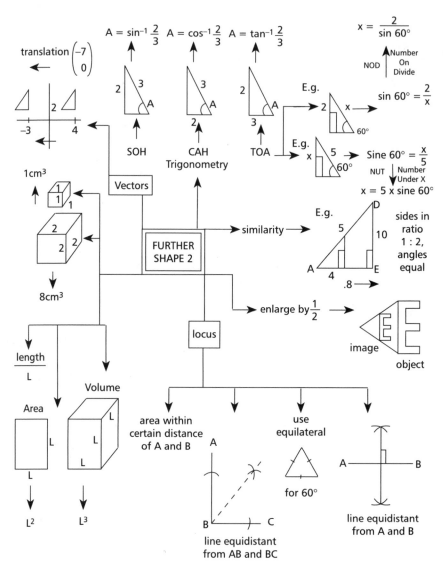

Maths mind-map 9

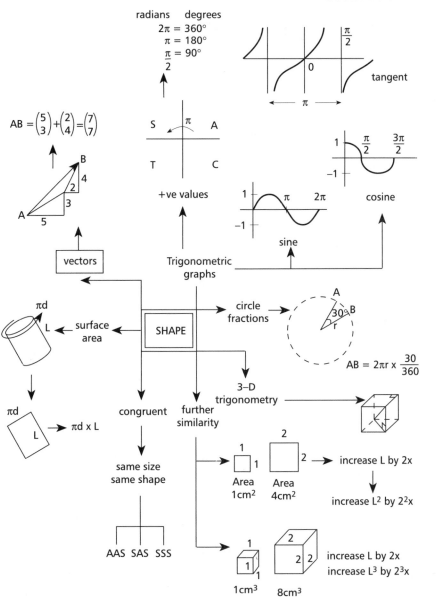

radians   degrees
$2\pi = 360°$
$\pi = 180°$
$\dfrac{\pi}{2} = 90°$

$\dfrac{\pi}{2}$

0

tangent

π

$AB = \begin{pmatrix} 5 \\ 3 \end{pmatrix} + \begin{pmatrix} 2 \\ 4 \end{pmatrix} = \begin{pmatrix} 7 \\ 7 \end{pmatrix}$

S π A

T   C

+ve values

B

4

2

3

A   5

1   $\dfrac{\pi}{2}$ $\dfrac{3\pi}{2}$

-1

cosine

1   π 2π

-1

sine

vectors

Trigonometric
graphs

πd

L

surface
area

SHAPE

circle
fractions

A

30 B

r

$AB = 2\pi r \times \dfrac{30}{360}$

πd

L

$\pi d \times L$

congruent

further
similarity

3–D
trigonometry

same size
same shape

AAS SAS SSS

1

1

Area
$1cm^2$

2

2

Area
$4cm^2$

increase L by 2x

2

increase L^2 by 2^2x

1

1   1

$1cm^3$

2

2   2

$8cm^3$

increase L by 2x
increase L^3 by 2^3x

Maths mind-map 10

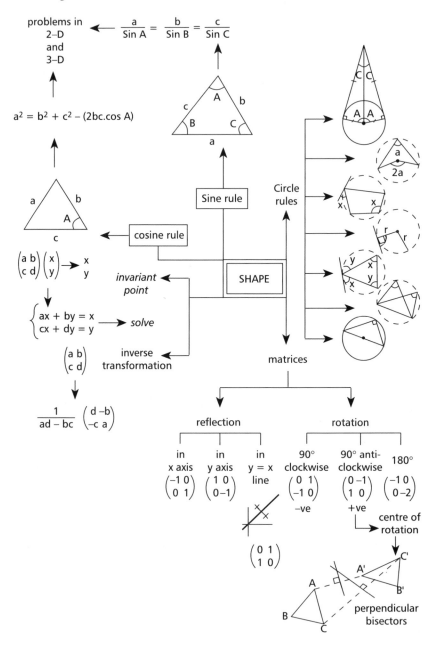

Maths mind-map 11

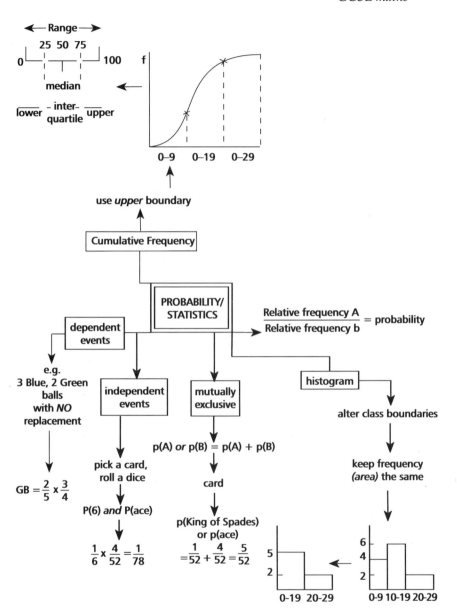

Maths mind-map 12

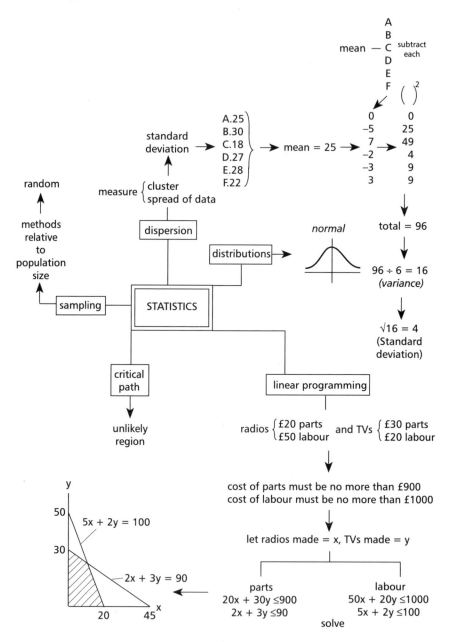

Maths mind-map 13

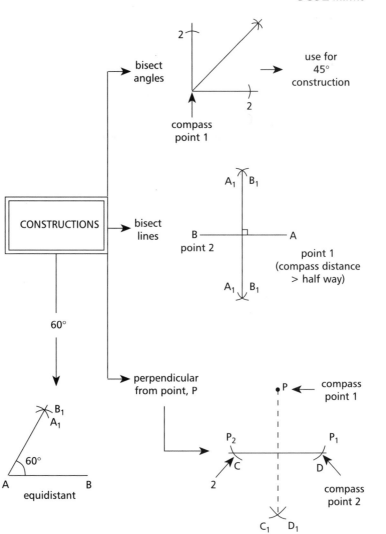

Maths mind-map 14

MATHS: WORKED EXAMPLES

1 Of a group of 22 men, 16 are over or equal to 25, 14 are married, 2 are under 25 and unmarried. How many are *over* 25 and married?

Solution

The use of Venn diagrams for dissection is confusing because facts cannot easily be linked up. Using a map, first, what is *known* can be put in:

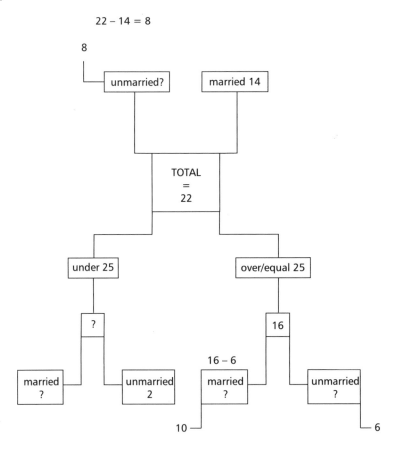

Unmarried: 8–2=6 (see top)

Over 25 and married: 16–6=10

The answer is 10.

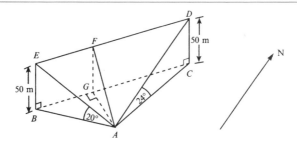

The figure represents a model of a hillside *ADE*.
ABC lies in the horizontal plane and *BCDE* lies in the vertical plane.
BE = *CD* = 50 metres.
Going due West from *A*, the slope of the hill is 20°.
Going due North from *A*, the slope of the hill is 24°.

(a) **(i)** I walk from *A* to *E*. Calculate the horizontal distance, *AB*, I have travelled.

$$\text{Sine } 20° = \frac{50}{AF} \rightarrow NUTI\ NOD \rightarrow$$
$$NUMBER\ ON\ TOP\ DIVISION \rightarrow AE = \frac{50}{\text{Sin } 20°}$$

(ii) If I walk from *A* to *D*, how far horizontally have I travelled?

$$A\ to\ D\ is\ A\ to\ C\ horizontally$$
$$\tan 24 = \frac{50}{AC} \rightarrow AC = \frac{50}{\tan 24°}$$

(b) Calculate the size of the angle *ABC*.

$$AC\ is\ North\ of\ AB\ (given)\ So$$
$$\angle ABC = \tan^{-1} \frac{AC}{AB}$$

The line *AG* is at right angles to the line *BC*.

(c) Calculate the length of *AG*.

$$\text{Sine } \angle ABC = \frac{AG}{AB} \rightarrow AG = AB \times \text{Sine} \angle ABC$$

AF is the line of greatest slope of the hillside.

(d) Calculate the distance *AF*.

$$GF = CD = EB = 50m$$
$$GF^2 + AD^2 = AF^2 \rightarrow 50^2 + AD^2 = AF^2$$

Two fair coins are tossed together.

$$\begin{array}{c} \text{Coin 1} \\ \underset{2}{\text{Coin}}\ \begin{array}{cc} HH & HT \\ TH & TT \end{array} \end{array}$$

(a) What is the probability that the result is

    (i) both heads?

$$\frac{1}{4}$$

    (ii) either both heads or both tails?

$$\frac{2}{4} = \frac{1}{2}$$

(b) Two biased coins are tossed together. For one coin the probability it will land heads is p and for the other coin the probability it will land heads is q.

    (i) What is the probability that they will both land heads?

$$p.q$$

    (ii) What is the probability that they will land either both heads or both tails?

$$pq + (1-p)(1-q)$$

$$\begin{array}{c} \text{Coin 1 } (p) \\ \begin{array}{ccc} & H & T \\ \underset{2}{\text{Coin}}\ H & pq & (1-p)q \\ (q)\ \ T & p(1-q) & (1-p)(1-q) \end{array} \end{array}$$

For testing purposes, a robot car is driven into a concrete wall.
The variation of speed with time is shown by the graph below.

(i) After how many seconds did the car reach its maximum speed?

.... *15 secs*

(ii) In reaching its maximum speed, what was the car's average acceleration expressed in ft/s².

Join O to A $\frac{88}{15}$ *ft/s²*

(iii) After how many seconds was the car's actual acceleration equal to its average acceleration? Explain how you arrived at your answer.

.... *Draw tangent parallel to OA*

.... *8 seconds*

(iv) Explain how you could use the graph to estimate the distance travelled by the car.

Find the area beneath the graph (D=SxT)
Each large square is 100 ft

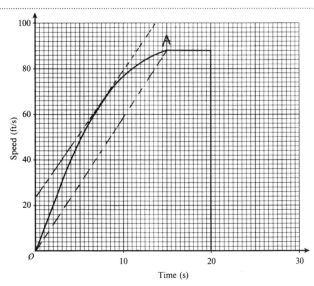

$A'B'C'$ is the image of ABC under an enlargement with scale factor k.

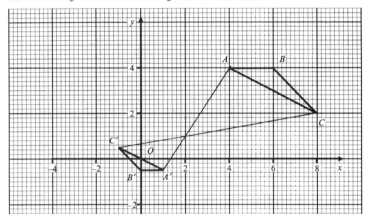

(a) What is the value of the scale factor k?

$$k = \frac{1}{2}$$

(b) Give the coordinates of the centre of enlargement.

$$\left(2, 1\right)$$

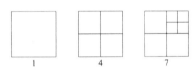

| 1 | 4 | 7 |

To form the sequence of drawings shown above, the first square is quartered, then the top right hand square of each drawing is quartered.

The number under each drawing shows the number of empty squares that can be counted.

(a) If the sequence is continued, how many squares can be counted

    (i) in the 4th drawing? 10

    (ii) in the 10th drawing? 28

    (iii) in the nth drawing? .... $3n-2$

(b) (i) Find a square number, s, between 9300 and 9500.

$$97 \times 97 =$$

    (ii) Which drawing contains s empty squares?

$$3n - 2 =$$

$$n = \frac{+2}{3} =$$

RST is the tangent at S to the circle with centre O.

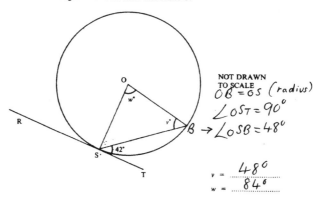

NOT DRAWN
TO SCALE

$OB = OS$ (radius)

$\angle OST = 90^\circ$

$\to \angle OSB = 48^\circ$

$v = \dfrac{48^\circ}{}$

$w = \dfrac{84^\circ}{}$

Solve the equation $4x^2 - 29x - 24 = 0$.

$$(4x + 3)(x - 8) = 0$$
$$x - 8 = 0 \quad , \quad 4x + 3 = 0$$
$$x = 8 \qquad x = -\frac{3}{4}$$

A girl made a light wooden frame in the form of a cube measuring 20 cm × 20 cm × 20 cm.
To make it more rigid, she tied wire from B to D and from B to E.

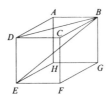

Calculate the angle between the two pieces of wire.

$$DB^2 = CB^2 + DC^2 = 800 \to DB = \sqrt{800} = 20\sqrt{2}$$

$$\angle DBE = \tan^{-1} \frac{20}{20\sqrt{2}} = \tan^{-1} \frac{1}{\sqrt{2}}$$

FURTHER MATHS EXAMPLES

1 Calculate the probability that an operation will fail twice, given that it has a 60 per cent success rate first time. If it is unsuccessful it can be repeated, now with a success rate of 30 per cent.

2 Draw a tree-diagram or use a tabulation to show outcomes of tossing a coin three times.

3 Calculate the distance between 2 ships, 30 miles apart, if they move at constant speeds in direction 060° and 100°, ship A moving at 20km/h, ship B at 24km/h.

4 Draw the graphs of $y = 10\sin x^0$, $y = 6$ and $10y + x = 50$. Use these to solve $5\sin x = 3$ and $100\sin x = 50 - x$.

five

GCSE English language and literature

This chapter aims to cover completely all aspects necessary for success in both GCSE English language and English literature. It includes mind-mapping and mnemonics to cover the following essential areas:

1 *Standard English* – punctuation, grammar and spelling.
2 *Course-work* – in both English language and English literature, including selected set texts.
3 *Oral skills*
4 *The examination syllabuses* – with worked examples.

GCSE English is not an 'easy' option. Maths is highly abstract in the main and science is full of difficult concepts; for GCSE there is a limited number of themes or mental 'files' you need to commit to memory. However, in English the task of learning is virtually endless. At no point can you say, 'I know all my English.' Perhaps you can be competent in punctuation and grammar, and be highly proficient at dissecting key words from a comprehension piece or analysing a Shakespeare play, but the process of creativity never ends. As a teacher of maths, science and English and a writer of fiction (the books and TV series of *Samson Superslug*) I can find satisfaction in the relatively finite knowledge needed for science and maths and also the endless diversity necessary for creative work in English.

Basically, the difficulty with English, therefore, is that there is so much to learn. You can learn *general* strategies of how to write a creative piece (e.g. a story), how to respond to a question on Romeo and Juliet or an informative piece of writing: but there is not a finite number of patterns to learn, as there are for science and maths GCSE. However, such general knowledge at your fingertips, for use in course-work and exams and set books and course-work text for GCSE, *can* be set out in mind-map form for question-related areas, e.g. 'Discuss the character of Lady Macbeth.' The rules of spelling and grammar can also be mind-mapped and mnemonics created for awkward individual words.

The greatest problems that GCSE English students seem to have include the following:

a They have difficulty writing good, well-structured stories.
b Even good pupils have 'blind spots' concerning the spelling of some words and punctuation can be scrappy.
c There is confusion over what constitutes 'good writing'. Students are in good company here – critics and publishers' editors cannot agree with each other! However, a certain formal style of writing works best in GCSE. (Being *too* creative might lead to failure – I'm sure that Roald Dahl and James Joyce would have raised a few frowns!) Unfortunately, sometimes teachers try to explain how to improve writing by saying, 'put in longer, more descriptive words', which can lead to often hilarious results.

Most English teachers (and examiners) prefer rather sober, well-constructed writing, well-punctuated with well-structured sentences and the knowledge of a few 'sophisticated' words – but *used in the right context*. If you pay attention to some of the writing in your literary texts (e.g. *Animal Farm, Lord of the Flies, A Kestrel for a Knave*) you will notice lines that strike you. In fact, some of the best lines in literature are not necessarily those with long words but those that convey the sense of a high *intelligence* in the writer and a deep *understanding* of *human nature*. When your teacher tells you to write about *feelings*, this is what they are asking for. Such understanding is at the root of good works, like those mentioned above or 'Adrian Mole', Shakespeare, Dickens and many others, regardless of genre.

All this involves writing and reading skills. For today's GCSE you will also need to be proficient in oral skills. (These are also valuable life skills – whatever job you end up doing.)

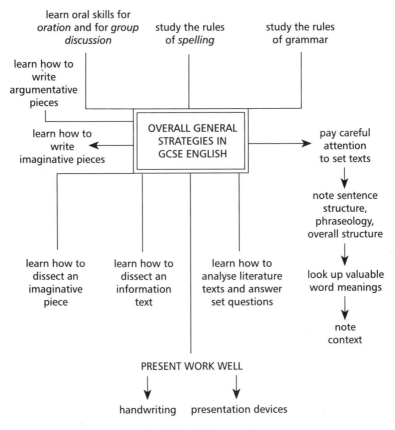

English mind-map 1

In order to succeed in English, the organization of your work, whatever the content, is of paramount importance. The structuring of a sentence, a paragraph or of the overall piece of work catches the eye of the reader, whether teacher or exam marker. It is also important to keep to the point or to the question. This is what gains the A or A*. You must ensure that everything that you write, every sentence, is well written, and that every word is spelt properly and in context. For course-work a word-spell (or spell-check) is invaluable but cannot replace a sound understanding of the way in which our spelling system works.

STORY WRITING

Mind-mapping is an excellent way of 'filming' *information* in English, of setting out the *structure* of a piece and is also a useful device for *brainstorming for ideas*.

If you wish to write a story, for example, you will need, first, to set down a *plot*. The following relates to a final story that achieved A+ in GCSE:

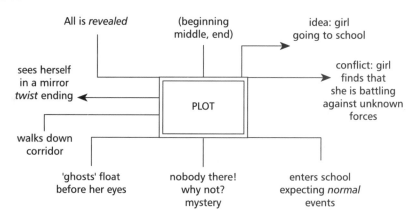

Mind-map for a specific plot

The story has a *beginning*, a *middle* and an ending (think of a good 'twist' at the end if possible). In a good story there should be a character that you can identify with – meaning that you should be aware of some of their thoughts, perhaps likes and dislikes. The character needs to be taken into *conflict* with others, the environment, supernatural forces, etc. You could introduce humour, suspense and a sense of the passing of time; but in a short story things should happen fairly quickly. Descriptive words are important but *only* as they support the action and in this context your central character should be 'active', 'throwing open a door' or 'dashing upstairs' rather than just *going* upstairs. If the central character is an old person their joints can 'creak with every step' not simply 'ache'. The resolution of the story can be quite short – it is a 'wrapping-up' exercise.

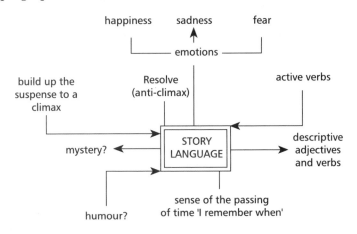

English mind-map 2

Writing is *hard work.* In course-work one writing or *draft* will not be enough. A high grade is only achieved by very careful editing of your own work. You will need to look at every sentence and ask yourself whether or not that is the *best* sentence that you can write. Do sentences link with each other to form a coherent paragraph? Do paragraphs link to form a coherent whole?

Dialogue is difficult. It must be natural, yet not *too* natural or 'slangy' (for GCSE – definitely no swearing).

Below is a story, with no dialogue, that gained A* recently.

Tina's story

Time Lapse
It was a bitterly cold autumn day. Rebecca pulled her coat about her and shivered as she padded along the leaf-strewn avenue

towards school. She was surprised at the sudden change in the weather. Yesterday it had been frosty, but sunny, and there had been a snap in the air that was exhilarating.

A sudden gust of wind sent the brown leaves scurrying across her path and snatched at her hair. She looked along the road towards the school, expecting to see the hordes of laughing chattering schoolgirls of yesterday with school jackets unbuttoned and the straps of satchels weighing down slender shoulders. There was no-one, not even Mrs Banks standing at the gates with folded arms, frowning beneath her beetle brows and carefully coiffured hairstyle. Where were they – yesterday's crowds? Where were the poking, prodding, giggling, teasing, happy soul mates, releasing their inhibitions before the deadly dull labours of the school day?

Rebecca walked on, feeling her knees creaking beneath the slight weight of her frame. Yesterday, she remembered, she had skipped along this street, full of hope for the future, a bundle of youthful energy ready to conquer the world. Today she felt weary, her limbs not responding to her urgent calls to be the athletic girl of yesterday. With every step her muscles complained.

Rebecca reached the school gate and stopped, feeling a little bewildered. The heavy iron gates of the school were closed, though not locked. She looked around her, missing the warmth of congenial company, hoping for the sight of a familiar face. It was not Saturday or Sunday, she was sure of that, yet the school grounds were completely empty, the borders overgrown, paths left unswept, the stonework and paint of the buildings faded.

She pushed at the heavy, iron gates, surprised at the effort needed to open them and bewildered by the flaking paint and ingrained rust on the metalwork. Yesterday, surely, these gates had been as clean as a whistle, newly painted green, a shocking colour but, with the neatly trimmed borders and newly mown lawns, giving the school an air of spruceness and elegance.

Wearily, Rebecca picked her way along the litter-strewn path to the school's main door. Tentatively, she pushed it open and revealed the long, familiar corridor, now carpetless and dusty. She stepped inside and stood for a moment, listening to the hollow silence, and then moved on towards the Great Hall. Where, where was everybody? Where were the furnishings of yesterday?

In the Great Hall she found a lone chair parked against a rear wall, half its back rest missing, and she sat down facing the stage. Yesterday, rows of bright-eyed, newly washed and polished schoolgirls had sat, still and silent, gazes fixed upon the stage. Today, there was just bleakness; a sad memorial to a great past. Suddenly, as she sat staring vacantly towards the empty stage ghostly forms began to appear – of row upon row of straight-backed seats, of teachers sitting on the fringes of a large audience of assembled girls, their attention focused as one on the tall, domi-neering figure of Miss Cudsworth, the Headmistress, her eyes beady behind horn-rimmed spectacles resting on the end of a harsh, beaked nose. Somewhere a girl giggled, and the ghostly Miss Cudsworth turned and barked a reproof, not as yesterday in recognizable living tones but as an absent form intoning from a distant cavern: 'Quiet girls!' the sounds lingering and echoing in the hall long after she had spoken.

Then, as quickly as the apparitions had appeared, they vanished, leaving Rebecca staring in bemusement at the empty hall, feeling a tingling of terror assail her spine.

She rose and walked across the floorboards, hearing her footfalls on the wood and engulfed by the lingering silence beyond her steps. Her mind refused to function anymore, unable to link what she saw with what she felt was real.

In a back corridor a mouse squeaked and ran across her path, reminding her that there was reality in the unreal. Then she stopped, and a new wave of panic engulfed her. At the end of the passage, barring her way, a small white-haired woman stood facing her. The woman's face was careworn and lined but her eyes blazed with a horror that was terrifying. For a moment, Rebecca stood transfixed and then, unaccountably, began to approach the apparition, drawn by some desire to know, to understand. She moved forward maybe ten steps then stopped again. Deep within her mind a glimmer of comprehension was developing.

She looked down at her hands. They were brown and wrinkled, exactly like the hands of the woman facing her. And then she knew. She knew that the apparition, the little old lady standing before her, was a reflection in a mirror on the end wall. The vision of the time-worn crone was no ghostly apparition, no supernatural demon sent to punish her. The little white-haired old lady was *her*!

Rebecca staggered. Realization of her infirmity suddenly weighed her down. She felt misery welling up like a flood within her. In one day she had aged from young vibrant schoolgirl to weak, suffering old age. Weakly, she staggered on and out of the back door into the swirling leaves of autumn, and stumbled along a path near the hockey fields, now heavy with long, uncut grass.

She stopped in front of a large sign that read:

St. Augustine's School for Girls
Independent Day School

but it was a faded sticker spread across one corner that caught her eye:
Closed February, 1944, due to economic circumstances.

Then she remembered. It had been fifty years since she had last attended St. Augustine's as a young, hopeful teenager. Now she was a widow of retirement age, suffering from inexplicable lapses of memory. Her life was not beginning, it was on its last lap.

She turned away from the sign and hobbled away down the path, a sad victim of Alzheimer's disease. She left the multicoloured leaves of October frisking across the decaying timbers of the school and disappeared back into the real world once again.

Narrative (in stories etc.) can be condensed in mind-map forms:

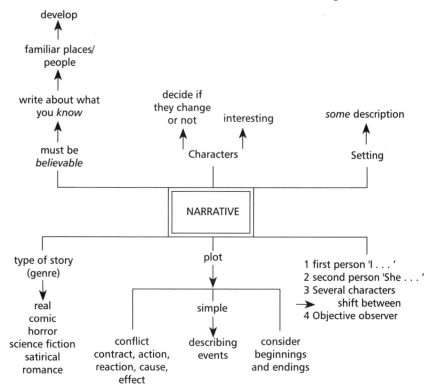

English mind-map 3

Care must be taken with dialogue:

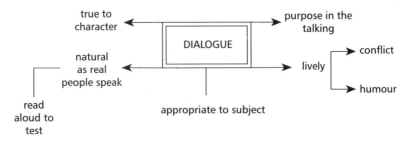

English mind-map 4

Make your beginnings eye-catching so that the reader's attention is attracted. For example:

It was his fault, wholly and solely his fault that they had missed the train. (Katherine Mansfield)

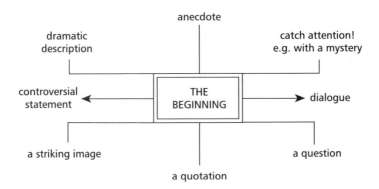

English mind-map 5

The ending sentence (particularly in a short story) is also very important. For example:

(1) 'They both were silent once more.'
(2) '. . . And he handed her an egg.' (Katherine Mansfield)

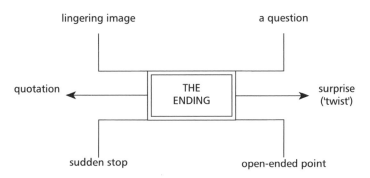

English mind-map 6

Images created in the mind of the reader are important. Charles Dickens is the master of creating images through his writing. At the end of *A Tale of Two Cities* the evil Carton 'reforms' and sacrifices himself on the guillotine for another and we are left with the lingering image of this man, standing on the scaffold. It makes you want to weep!

> It is a far, far better thing that I do, than I have ever done; it is a far, far better rest that I go to, than I have ever known.

To write well you need first to create a *picture* in your mind of what you wish to write about. This applies to all forms of writing, and seeing a video or film can make the image more concrete – even for abstract ideas. When you have created the image in your mind, do a rough mapping of the image. It will help you to link key words and ideas within a paragraph. Lesley, whom I tutored for GCSE English, was a pupil whose writing had no life until she saw the film of a book she needed to write about. Suddenly, she was able to translate abstract words from a book to concrete images in her mind to abstract words in her essay.

Technique is important. The writing can, for example, become tedious if sentences are all the same length (see mind-map 7).

There is no rigid prescription here. Practice gives a 'feel' for what is right.

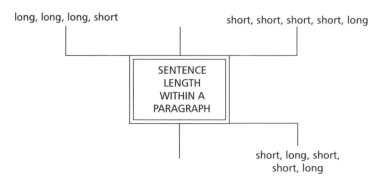

English mind-map 7

To make the image as complete as possible for the reader you will need to *describe* the characters (where possible within the context of the story) and the environment (room, street, countryside) *without* making the story drag.

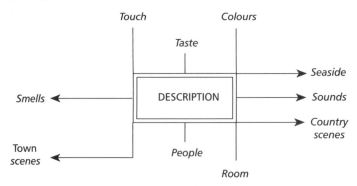

English mind-map 8

USING MIND-MAPS FOR BRAINSTORMING

Whether for course-work or in an exam, setting aside a few minutes for brainstorming around a set question for ideas can be invaluable. It will improve your English to a high level for set texts in literature as well as for argumentative or creative exercises. The reason for this is that brain-storming about a central theme initiates a search throughout *all* the avenues of the mind for related information and ideas. Obviously, not all this information and ideas will be relevant, but you will find within your own mind *so much* you can use, that you will need to *select*. (Although for informative writing you may need first to research the relevant texts and *then* brainstorm.) For example, the character of Ralph in *Lord of the Flies* can be laid out in this form:

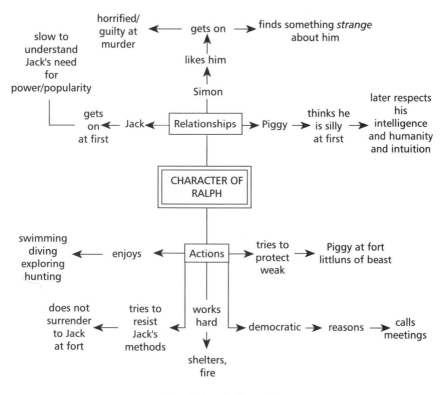

English mind map 9

BOOK AND POETRY ANALYSIS

Specific set and suggested texts for exam and course-work are analysed with mind-mapping at the end of this chapter. A general analysis of a book should include the following:

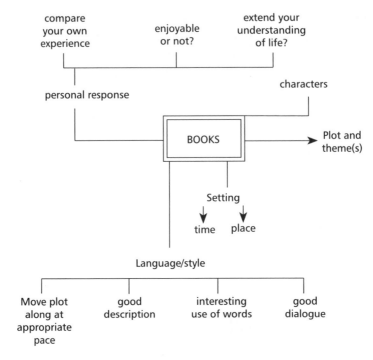

English mind-map 10

Each of the above can be broken down into further subdivisions which can be mind-mapped (e.g. theme or themes).

The analysis of poetry can also be mapped as shown in mind-map 11 on the following page.

ARGUMENTATIVE PIECES

Another form of writing that you will need to employ is *argument*. Argumentative writing is greatly enhanced by displaying points clearly. Laying out points in mind-map form allows you:

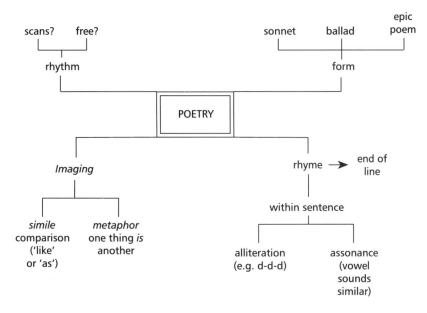

English mind-map 11

a To check easily that you have included *all* points.
b To be able to organize the argument effectively.

There are several ways of presenting this form of essay, depending on the question. For example:

1 Simply present the side you believe in as forcibly as possible.
2 Present both sides of the coin and then conclude with your opinion.

In such a form of writing you need to bear the following points in mind – see mind-map 12 on the next page.

In argument you will need to *empathize* with the views of those who have opinions. However *you* feel you will need to be able to visualize yourself as, for example, a racist, an extreme right-winger or an egalitarian politically-correct left-winger! However much in disagreement you may be with a person or group, to argue effectively you will need to be able to argue *their* side and then be able to counter their arguments effectively.

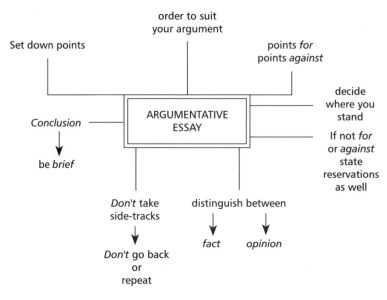

English mind-map 12

COMPREHENSION

Comprehension forms a large part of your English course. It is a test of your understanding of what you read and satisfies the demands of GCSE and National Curriculum assessment that Reading is tested extensively as well as Writing. At the heart of Reading are word meanings but also sense or context. For example:

In context   'The fox jumped over the gate.'
Out of context   'The gate jumped over the fox.'

Skimming

When you read in a normal manner you 'skim' for meaning, picking out *key* phrases and words. This works satisfactorily as long as you recognize those words and phrases and can interpret them easily. It is a simple matter then to pick them out and arrange them in *mind-map* form.

However, if the passage includes words and phrases about which you are unsure, you cannot allot them a place in your scheme as important parts of the passage, or as merely irrelevant elements. Practice with exam *anthologies* gives good preparation in sorting the 'wheat' from the 'chaff' and this is done for you in the worked examples at the end of this chapter. In general, the process of analysis should proceed as follows:

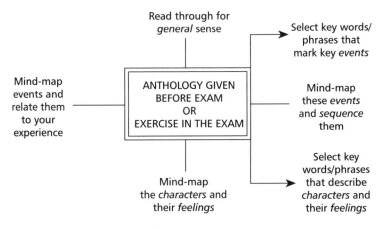

English mind-map 13

This process should cover most questions that are asked on the *anthology* or *comprehension* for exams or as assignment work.

ORAL WORK

Speaking and listening assessment occupies a large proportion of course-work.

There are several aspects of speaking that need to be attended to: see mind-map 14 on the next page.

Even when 'just' reading you will need to employ many techniques to achieve the highest grade. Practice in these techniques is *essential*: see mind-map 15 overleaf.

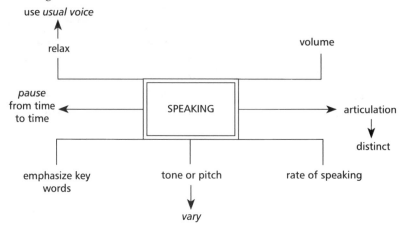

English mind-map 14

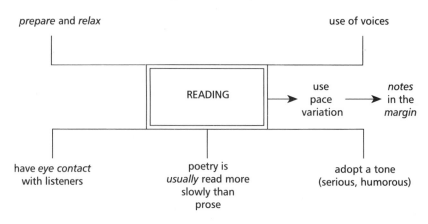

English mind-map 15

Similarly, for a group discussion you will need to consider various elements; as can be seen in mind-map 16 overleaf.

Oral skills can be summed up as follows in mind-map 17 on the next page.

The more you can *visualize* what you are talking about the more visual will your language become and the clearer will be the *picture* that you create in your listeners' minds. The memorizing of *keywords* and *ideas* for a talk will make that talk 'flow' and gain a high grade.

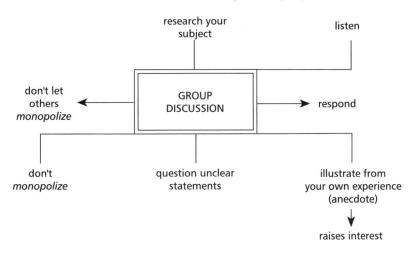

English mind-map 16

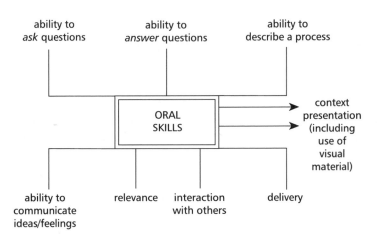

English mind-map 17

A typical talk (or essay) subject is 'smoking' and key themes include the following, as seen in mind-map 18 on the following page.

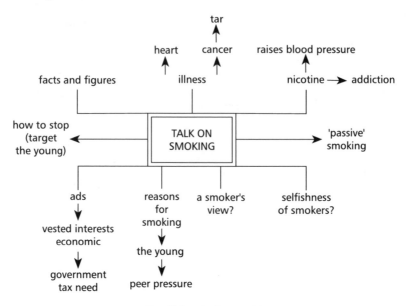

English mind-map 18

MAPPING THE GENERAL FEATURES OF SPELLING

In order to achieve top grades in English, what you spell must be *perfect*. You can use a word-spell for course-work, but you will need to commit to memory the basic rules for examinations. The two mind-maps which follow (maps 19 and 20) detail a learning system of fundamental rules.

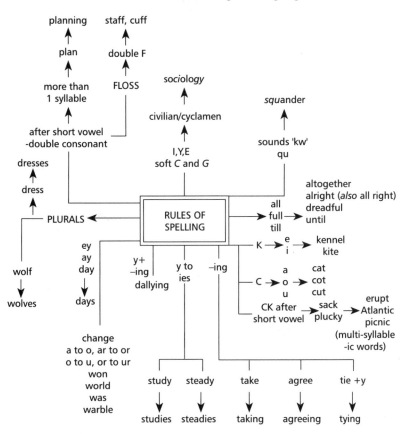

planning   staff, cuff
    ↑   ↑
  plan   double F
    ↑   ↑
more than   FLOSS   soci*o*logy
1 syllable   ↑
    ↑   civilian/cyclamen   *squ*ander
after short vowel   ↑   ↑
-double consonant   I,Y,E   sounds 'kw'
                        soft *C* and *G*   qu
dresses   altogether
    ↑   alright (*also* all right)
  dress   all dreadful
    ↑   ┌─── RULES OF ───→   full → until
    ├─ PLURALS ← │ SPELLING │   till
            │   └───────────┘   K → e → kennel
    ey   i   kite
    ay
wolf day   y+   y to   –ing   C → a   cat
    ↓ ↓   –ing   ies   o → cot
wolves days dallying   u   cut
                                                              erupt
                                    CK after → sack → Atlantic
                                    short vowel plucky   picnic
    change   (multi-syllable
a to o, ar to or   -ic words)
o to u, or to ur
    won
  world   study steady   take   agree   tie +y
    was   ↓   ↓   ↓   ↓   ↓
  warble   studies steadies taking agreeing tying

English mind-map 19

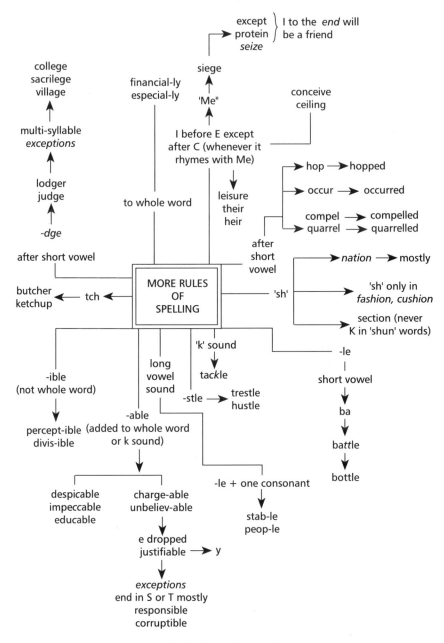

except ⎞ I to the *end* will
protein ⎠ be a friend
seize

siege

financial-ly
especial-ly

'Me"

conceive
ceiling

college
sacrilege
village

I before E except
after C (whenever it
rhymes with Me)

hop → hopped

occur → occurred

compel → compelled
quarrel → quarrelled

multi-syllable
exceptions

leisure
their
heir

to whole word

lodger
judge

nation → mostly

-*dge*

after short vowel

after
short
vowel

'sh' only in
fashion, cushion

butcher
ketchup ← tch ←

MORE RULES
OF
SPELLING

→ 'sh'

section (never
K in 'shun' words)

'k' sound

-le
|
short vowel

-ible
(not whole word)

long
vowel
sound

tackle

-stle → trestle
hustle

ba

percept-ible
divis-ible

-able
(added to whole word
or k sound)

battle

bottle

despicable
impeccable
educable

charge-able
unbeliev-able

-le + one consonant

e dropped
justifiable → y

stab-le
peop-le

exceptions
end in S or T mostly
responsible
corruptible

English mind-map 20

THE RULES OF PUNCTUATION AND GRAMMAR

One task of learning is to translate subject matter into easily *digestible* form which is therefore *understandable*. *Grammar* and *punctuation* are aspects of English that need to be learnt and, although much can be memorized through reading, accuracy is only achieved through *conscious* application to learning the processes and principles of structure. Without this knowledge your writing will be ineffective. In order to *understand* fully you need to *use* this knowledge in writing.

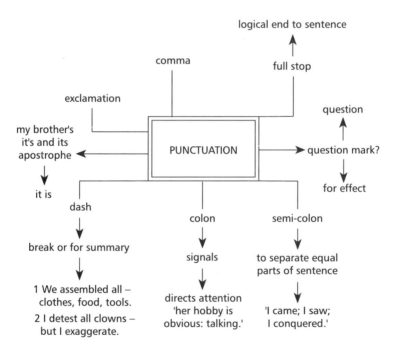

English mind-map 21

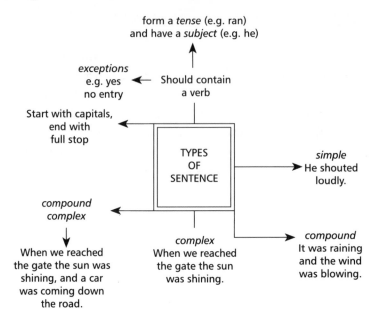

English mind-map 22

The comma is extremely important. A further 'file' is necessary to explain it.

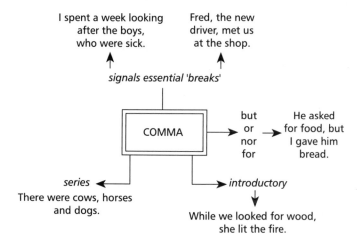

English mind-map 23

Knowing grammar includes knowing your tense and unfortunately many pupils that I encounter muddle up tense, switching from present to future. To *keep* the tense is vital for securing high grades.

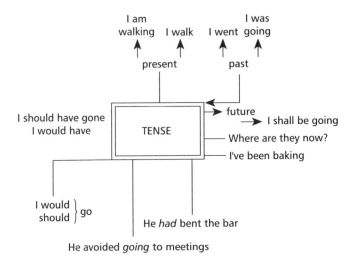

English mind-map 24

There are also a few rules for punctuation:

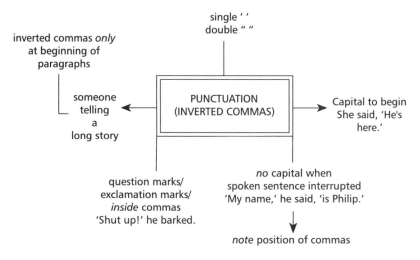

English mind-map 25

There are figures of speech that you will need to know about, especially for the analysis of poetry:

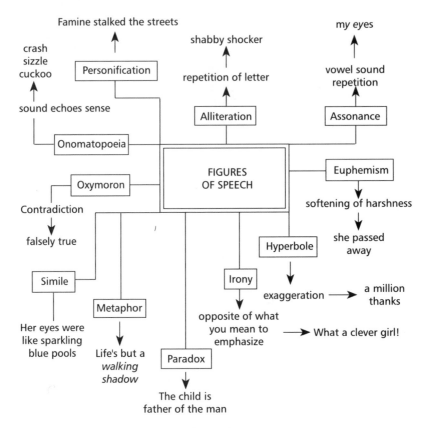

English mind-map 26

Some useful words and ideas for descriptive writing:

People

Figure tall, short, lanky, stout, thin, fat, frail, athletic, bent, manly, powerful, gigantic, deformed, dwarf-like, delicate

Head and face round, oval, long, small, thin, fat, flat, wrinkled

Nose long, fat, snub, straight, broad, dainty, enormous

Hair straight, wavy, curly, coarse, fine, tangled, brown, grey, blonde, silvery, ginger, auburn, black, golden, long, silky, bobbed, plaited

Eyes clear, bright, large, small, brown, blue, green, grey, shy, beady, shifty, twinkling, sparkling

Skin tanned, pale, swarthy, fair, bronzed, sunburnt, ruddy, rough, smooth, freckled

Mouth, lips, teeth wide, thin, rose-bud, twisted, stained, bad, decayed, irregular, projecting, uneven

Character kind, proud, vain, greedy, selfish, miserable, affection-ate, honest, humble, charming, spiteful, mean, loyal, generous, sincere, lovable, stubborn, obstinate, enthusiastic, timid, excitable, bold, impetuous

Clothing shirt, collar, tie, trousers, shorts, pants, bathing suit, shoes, socks, pyjamas, jumper, sweater, suit, jacket, overcoat, vest, blouse, dress, skirt, high heels, boots, stockings, tights, hat, cap, scarf, cuffs, gloves

Habits and characteristics drumming fingers, spitting, sniffing, coughing, putting one's head on one side, peering, quizzical, worried, troubled, smirking, laughing, giggling, sneering, limp-ing, finger sucking, blinking, twitching, tapping a foot, upright, smart, ragged, untidy, dowdy, stroking chin/beard, brushing back hair, pulling an ear

Voice low, high-pitched, squeaky, shrill, hoarse, deep, harsh, grating, rasping, tenor, bass, pleasant, husky, nasal, quavering

Movement quick, slow, laboured, walking, running, leaping, clapping, writing, drawing, painting, washing, dusting, stroking, smacking, hitting, hanging, sawing, chopping

Sounds

Birds singing, chirping, whistling, hooting, fluttering, chattering, cawing

People shouting, crying, weeping, laughing, screaming, shrieking, tutting, giggling, groaning, moaning, muttering, whistling, singing, hum of voices

Nature leaves rustling, thunder clapping, rain beating and pattering, wind rushing, stream rushing, steam hissing, brook bubbling, water dripping/dribbling/gushing/rushing, mice squeaking, bees humming/buzzing, dogs barking, cats mewing, cows lowing, sheep bleating, horses neighing, lions roaring, elephants trumpeting

Things radio/television blaring out, tap dripping, crackling of a fire, things frying, bubbling of boiling water, clock ticking, door creaking

Smells flowers, roses, sweet peas, the farmyard, salt breeze, hot chestnuts, burnt toast, hot cakes, turkey in the oven, scent/perfume, old socks, onions, apples, bananas, strawberries, petrol, fish and chips

Taste sugar, salt, sweet, sour, bitter, acid, orange, fishy, fruity, meaty, tasty

Touch caress, gentle, stroke, fondle, smack, kiss, hug, squeeze, rub, punch, stab, pound, prod, poke

Colours green grass, green trees, red roses, yellow daffodils, blue sky, green/blue sea, yellow sand, rainbow, coloured flags, coloured dresses, ties and shirts, whitewashed walls, silver moon, golden sun, white clouds, coloured lights, hair colours, shoe colours, skin colours

Country scenes trees, fields, river, brook, geese, ducks, sparrows, cows, sheep, horses, farmyard, bull, goat, hills, marshes, oak, sycamore, holly, horse-chestnut, cones, fallen leaves, trout, pike, fishermen, church, thatched cottage, fête

Town scenes road, streets, traffic lights, shops, pavement, lamp-post, kerb, shop-window, town hall, market, stalls, supermarket, station, platform, train, library, café, buses, lorries, vans, taxis, policemen, umbrellas, department store, offices

Seaside sand, shore, waves, pier, fair, roundabouts, Big Wheel, rocks, cliffs, caves, fish, yachts, rowing boats, liners, hotel, boarding house, pebbles, sea breeze, deck chairs

A room shape, decoration, windows, ceiling, floor-covering, heating, lighting, furniture

ENGLISH LITERATURE

Some texts are used more frequently than others in school. Some are set texts with Exam Boards. Much used are the following:

A Kestrel for a Knave (Barry Hines)
Animal Farm (George Orwell)
Lord of the Flies (William Golding)
Romeo and Juliet (William Shakespeare)
Macbeth (William Shakespeare)
World War I poetry and prose (Various)

However, the techniques suggested in this chapter can be applied to *any* novel, *any* poem or *any* play (whether by Shakespeare or any other playwright). Mind-maps can be used to summarize the themes, characters and plot in any text. The examples of literary analysis which follow simply show what can be achieved through mind-mapping.

Themes

Most novels contain more than one theme. In *A Kestrel for a Knave* the themes may be summarized as in mind-map 27.

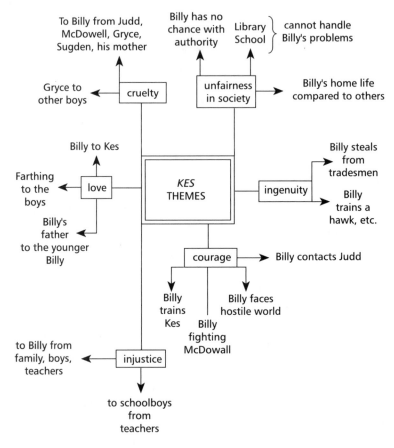

English mind-map 27

The themes in *Animal Farm* can similarly be dissected:

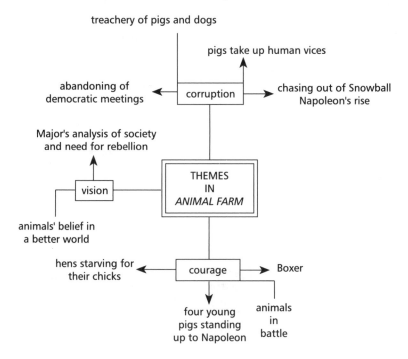

English mind-map 28

Behind the story in *Animal Farm* lies the history of the Russian Revolution (mind-map 29).

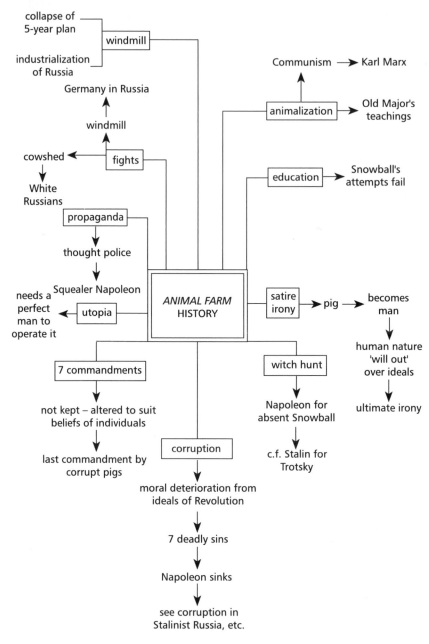

English mind-map 29

The characters of *Animal Farm* can be mapped out for clear filing in memory.

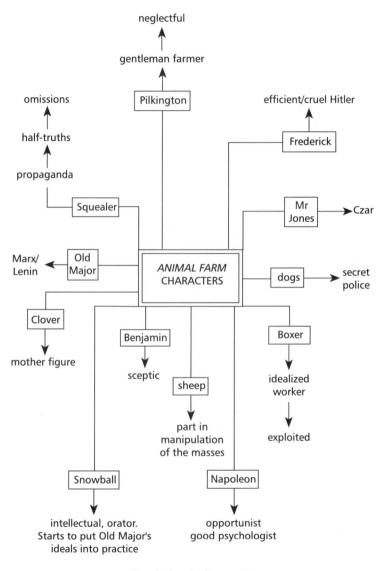

English mind-map 30

Sometimes the whole text can be summed up in a single mind-map,

with annotations. This gives an overall file for memory, which is useful
for comparisons with other texts.

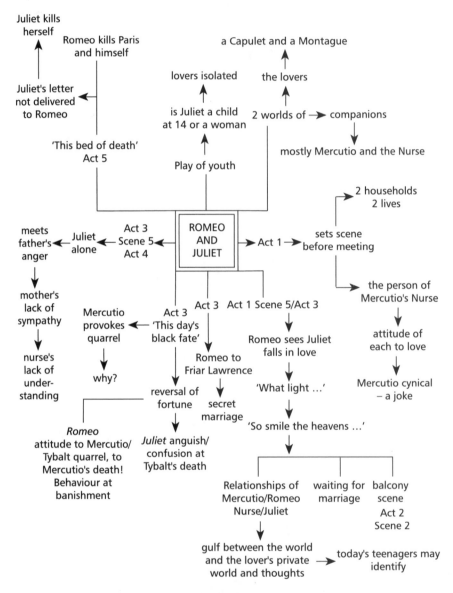

English mind-map 31

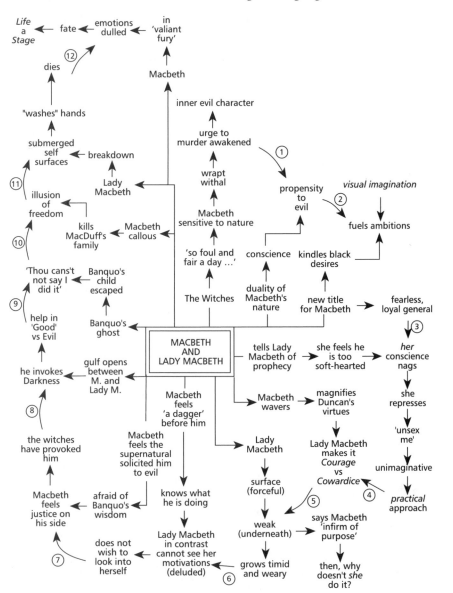

English mind-map 32

From *Macbeth* most questions are likely to revolve around the characters of Macbeth and Lady Macbeth, because they are by far the most powerfully drawn characters in the play. (See mind-map 32.)

Wilfred Owen's First World War poems are often used as a basis for English assignments.

English mind-map 33

Anthem for Doomed Youth

What passing bells for these who die as cattle?
Only the monstrous anger of the guns.
Only the stuttering rifles' rapid rattle
Can patter out their hasty orisons.
No mockeries now no prayers nor bells,
Nor any voices of mourning save the choirs –
The shrill, demented choirs of wailing shells;
And bugles calling for them from sad shires.

What candles may be held to speed them all?
Not in the hands of boys but in their eyes
Shall shine the holy glimmer of good-byes.
The pallor of girls' brows shall be their pall;
Their flowers the tenderness of patient minds.
And each slow dusk a drawing-down of blinds.

Wilfred Owen

'The Send-off' by Wilfred Owen is often used for comparison with 'Anthem for Doomed Youth', for the indication of *similarities* and *differences*.

The Send-off

Down the close darkening lanes they sang their way
To the siding-shed,
And lined the train with faces grimly gay.

Their breasts were stuck all white with wreath and spray
As men's are, dead.

Dull porters watched them, and a casual tramp
Stood staring hard,
Sorry to miss them from the upland camp.

Then, unmoved, signals nodded, and a lamp

Winked to the guard.

So secretly, like wrongs hushed-up, they went.
They were not ours:
We never heard to which front these were sent:

Nor there if they yet mock what women meant
who gave them flowers.

Shall they return to beating of great bells
In wild train-loads?
A few, a few, too few from drums and yells,
May creep back, silent, to village wells.
Up half-known roads.

Wilfred Owen

Owen's purpose in his poems was not pacifist or unpatriotic but to illuminate the discrepancy between the purpose of war (defence of territory or principle) and the means by which it is pursued (destruction of life and the setting aside of *other* principles).

Dulce Et Decorum Est

Bent double, like old beggars under sacks,
Knock-kneed, coughing like hags, we cursed through sludge,
Till on the haunting flares we turned our backs
And towards our distant rest began to trudge.
Men marched asleep. Many had lost their boots
But limped on, blood-shod. All went lame; all blind;
Drunk with fatigue; deaf even to the hoots
Of tired, outstripped Fifty-Nines that dropped behind.

Gas! Gas! Quick, boys! – An ecstasy of fumbling,
Fitting the clumsy helmets just in time;
But someone still was yelling out and stumbling,

And flound'ring like a man in fire or lime . . .
Dim, through the misty panes and thick green light,
As under a green sea, I saw him drowning.

In all my dreams, before my helpless sight,
He plunges at me, guttering, choking, drowning.

If in some smothering dreams you too could pace
Behind the wagon that we flung him in,
And watch the white eyes writhing in his face,
His hanging face, like a devil's sick of sin;

If you could hear, at every jolt, the blood
Come gargling from the froth-corrupted lungs,
Obscene as cancer, bitter as the cud
Of vile, incurable sores on innocent tongues, –
My friend, you would not tell with such high zest
To children ardent for some desperate glory,
The old Lie: *Dulce et decorum est*
Pro patria mori.

Wilfred Owen

There is no honour or glory here as the title suggests.

Many assignments are set as open-ended questions which will test
your ability to *think creatively*, to *argue a point* and also to *draw on your
own experience*. What do the poems say to us? What is your response to
them? Set out your initial maps in the above categories, and others, and
when you have decided on the *form* of your commentary, you can use
the facts and ideas from those brainstorming exercises.

An examiner's comment for candidates hoping to gain high grades (A
to A+) is revealing: 'Good ability to compare and *cross-reference wide
ranging material*, and make *personal interpretive judgments*.'

•

AN EXAMPLE OF COURSE-WORK

The following course-work examples were taken from the N.E.A.B. Standardizing materials (1994). Candidate B (Yvonne) achieved overall Grade A in her work.

Examiner's Comments

En1 (Speaking and Listening)

Bullying activity   Yvonne helpfully sets out the task for the group, then – in addition to her chairing role – is able to pick up and develop ideas from other group members. While concerned both to keep the discussion going and to move it on when necessary, she invites and welcomes contributions from others (although she might have made a greater direct effort to involve Russell). In her reading presentation she attempts eye-contact with the viewer, and there is some understated, but effective, characterization in her reading of the text.

Reading conference   Yvonne offers, largely unprompted, a detailed comparison between *To Kill a Mockingbird* and *Roll of Thunder, Hear My Cry* in terms of setting, character, theme and authorial viewpoint. Her ideas are expressed clearly and at some length, and she responds well to the teacher's questions. The vocabulary she uses is appropriate to the task, and she uses facial expression and tone both to emphasize what she is saying and to engage the interest of the other participant.

Poetry pairs   Having read through the poem with her partner, Yvonne quickly focuses on key words such as 'poison', and attempts to relate the situation in the poem to everyday life to make it understandable. Although not sure of the meanings of all archaic words (e.g. 'wiles'), she works hard at interrogating and explaining the implications of the imagery, involving her less certain partner in a detailed examination of the poem's impact, including an interesting consideration of the poet's 'conspiracy' with the sun.

Overall En1 assessment: 8+

In all three activities, Yvonne is secure at Level 8, as she contributes to a sustained group discussion, is 'able to express clearly and cogently points of view about complex matters' and can also 'interpret points of view with accuracy and discrimination'. Her ability to 'match language to context and purpose' is also sound, as is her awareness of the importance and function of non-verbal aspects of communication. Indeed, the sensitivity shown towards others in the group situations and the cogency of her presentation in the reading conference show qualities which lift the award.

En2 (Reading) and En3 (Writing)

Bullying in schools Yvonne reveals a detailed and responsive understanding of most of the tasks set, such as in the answers to Section A questions 1 and 6, and in Section B (where she shows awareness of how the arrangement of the writing affects the reader's response). There is a strong sense of audience in the Deputy Head's speech, which is well-organized and coherent despite an occasional awkwardness of expression; otherwise, expression is lucid and forceful, the vocabulary precise.

Discovery This compact, controlled and carefully-structured narrative achieves much in a short space: the sense of place, atmosphere, character and situation is powerful and convincing. Different time-scales are related, and actions are suggested rather than stated, creating a quietly subtle effect after the powerful opening which first engages the reader's attention. Small details, such as the wool snagged on the finger-nail, give a firm sense of reality to the story. The vocabulary and sentence-structure are sophisticated.

Elizabeth Proctor's memories of events in The Crucible In this response, Yvonne successfully exploits the possibilities of an empathetic response to literature, focusing consistently on feelings and motivation, and weaving in quotations and other references in a perfectly natural way. Although occasional clumsiness and technical errors intrude, the piece is sustained, fluent and well-structured; Yvonne uses language to capture a mood and tone which shows her awareness of Miller's attitudes and themes as well as of the interactions of his characters.

Overall En2 assessment: 9

These responses show Yvonne to be an intelligent, perceptive and responsive reader. She demonstrates implicit understanding of the effects of language in literary and non-literary texts, evaluates apparent and implicit meanings, and relates detail to 'the broader aspects of structure, content and style'. In the first response she makes 'effective use . . . of information gathered and used discriminately' from reference materials. Although the limited nature of the materials used precludes the award of the highest Level, Yvonne's achievement certainly fulfils the criteria.

Overall En3 assessment: 9–

All three responses show Yvonne's ability to produce 'sustained, committed and specific pieces of writing'; her material is well-organized and structured, and at its best (in 'Discovery') and parts of the work on 'The Crucible') is very assured indeed. Because of occasional clumsiness and loss of control, mostly in the first response but occasionally elsewhere, the award is put in the – subdivision.

English Literature

The poetry of Seamus Heaney   Despite its unnecessary length, which makes this become at times a 'naming of parts' response, this is a detailed and sharp exploration of Heaney's use of language. Yvonne shows understanding of the poet's themes, demonstrating both knowledge of, and sensitivity to, the apparent and implicit meanings of the poems. Her reflections are mature and convincing, but the number of texts analysed makes it difficult for Yvonne to write fluently or to establish an overview.

Elizabeth Proctor's memories of events in The Crucible   See the notes on En2/En3 above. This is a sophisticated response to character, plot, theme and language, offering sustained evidence of Yvonne's informed personal response to the drama and her confident ability to recreate material imaginatively is apparent.

A comparison of Roll of Thunder, Hear My Cry *and* To Kill a Mockingbird   Yvonne compares both texts well, within a fluent structure, which shows her skill in subtle and complex techniques. Once again, however, length becomes eventually counterproductive, leading to some raggedness towards the end, but this essay does compare themes, characters and viewpoints and demonstrates some awareness of the social context in its introduction.

Overall English Literature assessment: 9

There is no doubt that Yvonne can 'write clearly and sensitively about a range of texts, providing sustained evidence of informed personal response and showing an understanding of the effects of literary devices and structures used by a variety of writers'; in addition, she can compare texts, and evaluate apparent and implicit meanings, and is able to 'relate detail to the broader aspects of structure, content and style'.

Assignment

One of Candidate B's assignments follows.

Candidate B   *Assignment 11*

A Comparison of 'To Kill a Mocking Bird' and 'Roll of Thunder Hear My Cry'

Both *To Kill a Mocking Bird* and *Roll of Thunder Hear My Cry*, have similar backgrounds. The two novels are set in the 1930s in the southern states of America. Although each novel does not directly focus on it, the 'Wall Street Crash' had occurred in 1929 and there was a depression. Most people who were living in America at this time were deep in poverty and this was especially so for the Black American Citizens. Even though slavery had ended due to the American Civil War of 1861–1865 the black citizens still suffered. They had basically no legal rights because of the hatred they were subjected to by the white American people. In the south in the 1930s, segregation laws had been passed resulting in the inferior treatment of black people. Conditions were almost as bad as those in the times of slavery.

Each novel focuses on the exposure of the intolerance shown by the white people towards black people, how their irrational

---

hatred was expressed and how the families described within each novel were affected.

The protagonists in the two novels have many similarities. Both are young girls, in *To Kill a Mocking Bird* there is Jean Louise Finch, known as Scout, and in *Roll of Thunder Hear My Cry* there is Cassie Logan. Both of these characters tell the story of the novel. So there is a clear parallel that both books are first-person narratives but more importantly they are written from a child's perspective, be it Cassie's or Scout's. Both girls begin as very naïve characters, although bright at school, but throughout each novel it is clearly shown – by the way they as characters describe events in the novel – that they are learning, growing up and losing their 'child-like' innocence.

The central family in each novel has certain similarities with each other in their structure. Each has an educated member, Atticus Finch and Mama Logan are both professional people. Atticus is a lawyer and Mama is a school teacher. Both Cassie and Scout also have a wise father figure. Atticus in *To Kill a Mocking Bird* and Papa in *Roll of Thunder Hear My Cry* are both highly respected people within their communities. Atticus, because he is a lawyer, and Papa because of his independent status. A black family, economically stable as the Logans were, was not usual in the South in the 1930s. The Logans, unlike the majority of black families, were not share croppers; they were fortunate enough to have their own land, which they were very proud of. The fact that they were self sufficient and did not have to rely directly on white people, which most other families did through no fault of their own, made Papa a pillar of the community.

Throughout *Roll of Thunder Hear My Cry* Cassie's father seeks to instil pride in his children. He does not want his family to convince themselves that they are inferior to white people as many black people at that time did. After horrendous amounts of prejudice by the white people many black people had given up.

Cassie's father, by teaching his children, manages to make them believe in themselves and to be proud of who they are. Cassie's family were independent, Cassie knew that but she didn't understand the importance of it. Cassie did not realize that owning the land gave her a home of her own, she needed nothing from the white people, she would be as powerful if not more powerful than some white people. Thus therefore giving the Logans equal status to the white people, a status they hated but to themselves it gave dignity, dignity white people were permanently trying to take away from them and any other black family. Cassie's father shared his wisdom with her,

> All that belongs to you. You ain't never had to live on nobody's place but your own and long as I live and the family survives, you'll never have to. That's important.

Although at this stage in the novel Cassie had no clear comprehension of her father's message, throughout the novel she begins to appreciate it and she begins to learn even more from her parents and things she experiences.

For Cassie growing up is much more difficult than for Scout, her father has to explain to her things that are much more disturbing. She must learn these things from her father in order to prepare her for adulthood. Papa has to teach Cassie about prejudice and the only way he is able to do this is by describing the horrific past black people have to endure. For a child of Cassie's age this would be difficult to appreciate. When Papa tells the children not to go up to the Wallace store he only gives the children superficial reasons why, he says, 'There's drinking up there and I don't like it and I don't like them Wallaces either.' Even though they didn't understand the full reason, they said they would not go. They did though and on the realization of how serious it was, they confessed. Mama's punishment for disobeying their father and herself showed what the Wallaces did and how they treated the black people, thus explaining the reasons why they should not have gone to the store. Mama took them to visit Mr Berry. He had been a victim of a burning carried out by the Wallaces and as a result he was badly disfigured. Showing the children how Mr Berry's life had been totally destroyed by the Wallace's inhumanity towards the black people clearly showed them why they were not to go to the Wallace store. This was a very painful realization for Cassie to cope with and they were told that the fight between T.J. and Stacey lowered the Black race down to the expectations of the white people. Families, such as the Wallaces, treated the black people as animals. All Stacey and T.J. had succeeded in doing was giving the Wallaces ammunition about black families. Although if two white boys had fought nothing would be said, but to the Wallaces witnessing such a brawl would prove their theory that black people were animals. Cassie and the other children had learned some very important things from this. They realized they should never disobey but they had also realized how cruel and brutal the world was. Instead of the punishment being merely a whipping they had gained vital lessons from their mistakes.

Atticus also wishes to teach Scout valuable things that will assist her as she grows up. Atticus shares his wisdom with Scout in a very subtle way, as will become evident later. *To Kill a Mocking Bird* treats the delicacy of growing up very carefully but due to the different situation, the fact that the Logans are black in *Roll of Thunder Hear My Cry* the process of growing up is expressed as turbulent and much more difficult than the relatively smooth lives that are led by Scout and Jem Finch.

Both Scout and Cassie have an older brother who has a greater level of maturity than them. Scout's brother, Jem, and Cassie's brother, Stacey, with their more adult manner focus the reader's attention on the child-like innocence of each girl. Whilst trying to expose the hypocrisy and prejudices of the people in the American South in the 1930s, Harper Lee and Mildred Taylor both use children who are too young to appreciate or understand fully events that are taking place. Both books are written from a child's point of view and this technique is used to expose the hypocritical attitudes of people. This is possibly because children don't lie and society has not had the chance to force opinions on them. Children say what they want when they want, making the adult reader aware of the hypocrisy.

In *To Kill a Mocking Bird* there is a scene outside the jail-house where the entirely normal behaviour of Scout makes the people involved appreciate the ridiculous way in which they are acting. Atticus was sitting outside the jail-house where Tom Robinson was being held, when he was confronted by a group of men, some of them friends of his. The men, quite obviously to the adult reader, were there to kill Tom Robinson but to the child onlooker, Scout, the seriousness of the situation was unapparent. Scout's inquisitive nature prompted her to launch herself into the middle of the group of men and realizing that she knew one of the men, she began to chat with him. She continued the conversation in a child-like friendly manner which was natural to her. Without the appreciation of what she had managed to do, Scout had made Mr Cunningham aware of how absurd he was being. He was almost threatening a friend. Atticus knows of the detestation he had for Tom Robinson.

Scout also illuminated the illogical attitude of her school teacher to the reader. Although she only understood it as inconsistency of information. In school she was taught about Hitler and his inhuman treatment of the Jews. One evening whilst talking to Jem she unknowingly shows the irony in the attitude of the teacher.

> She went on today about how bad it was him treating the Jews like that, Jem, it's not right to persecute anybody, is it? . . .
> Well, coming out of the court-house that night, Miss Gates was – she was going down the steps in front of us, you musta not seen her – she was talking with Miss Stephanie Crawford. I heard her say it's time somebody taught 'em a lesson,

they were gettin' way above themselves . . . Jem, how can
you hate Hitler so bad an' then turn around and be ugly
about folks right at home?

Without realizing it, Scout highlighted the prejudiced attitude of
the teacher towards the black people in Maycombe.

Cassie, being a child, also shows the absurdity of what happens
whilst in Strawberry. Firstly, on arrival in Strawberry, Cassie did
not understand why they had to park their wagon far back behind
the white people's wagons. Then the next incident took place in
the Barnett Mercantile shop. Mr Barnett was serving them but
every time a white person came into the store he pushed them
aside and served the white customer. Cassie, being naive to the
situation, confronted Mr Barnett; in doing this Cassie caused a lot
of trouble for herself. To Mr Barnett and the other white people in
the shop she was a second-class citizen, a black person, to them,
had no right to question the action of a white person. As a result of
this Cassie was humiliated. Mr Barnett treated Cassie as if she was
some kind of object. Finally Cassie is very hurt that she is forced to
step off the pavement in order that a girl of her own age could
walk past. Cassie believed that she had as much right to walk
along the pavement as Lillian Jean, which she did; Lillian Jean was
no adult. Cassie highlighted the prejudices unknowingly and she,
unlike her family, did not see why they should accept such treatment. To Cassie black people were the same as white people. Her
day in Strawberry destroyed any belief in her young mind that life
was fair. She had to accept the painful realization that she was
going to be treated as a second-class citizen. Using these situations
the author, but using the child character, very clearly illustrates
how unfairly the black people were treated.

As explained briefly before, the innocence and youth of both
Cassie and Scout is highlighted by their older brother's greater
capacity for understanding. In *Roll of Thunder Hear My Cry* Cassie
cannot appreciate why Stacey tells Mama that he had been to the

Wallace Store and had been involved in a fight. When Mr Morrison discovered the children at the store he said he was not going to tell Mama but he wanted Stacey to explain to her. Stacey was not forced to, but he said he would. Unlike her brother Cassie believed that if they did not tell Mama it would be the end of the matter, but Stacey was adult enough to realize he owed it to his mother to tell her – his adult conscience prompted him into it.

In *To Kill a Mocking Bird*, Jem is shown to be a much more sensitive character than Scout. This is because he is maturing and therefore understanding things that appear complex to Scout. Chapter seven of the novel shows an example of this. Mr Nathan Radley cemented the knot hole in the tree. Using this knot hole the children had been receiving gifts and thus building up a friendship between, what was obvious to the reader, Boo Radley and themselves. Jem is aware of the connection between the gifts and Boo, and when the knot hole was cemented over, unlike Scout, he could see into the situation and realize that Nathan Radley had purposely destroyed Boo's effort to communicate with them. Jem appreciated how sad this was and he cried. This showed that he appreciated the misery of Boo's life.

Another incident involving Boo Radley shows this. On the evening of the fire that destroyed Miss Maudie's house Boo Radley made another attempt to secretly communicate with Jem and Scout. He unknowingly to them put a blanket around them. When Atticus confronted the children about where the blanket had come from they did not know. It was not until Jem thought about it that he realized it was Boo who put it there. When Atticus suggested returning the blanket Jem told him everything, 'omitting nothing, knot-hole, pants and all'. Throughout this Scout had not realised it was Boo who had put the blanket there, but she had also not understood why Jem told his father all their secrets. Scout also misinterpreted the fact when Atticus stopped Jem from continuing, whilst explaining their secrets. She could, as a child, only see that Atticus had not understood what Jem had said. Really though

Atticus could appreciate the point of Jem; Boo would be punished if the blanket was returned. It is clear that Scout only had a superficial understanding of the situation.

As explained previously Scout and Cassie learn a lot from their fathers. One recurring point is mentioned throughout *To Kill a Mocking Bird* and each time Scout grasps a further understanding of it. Primarily Atticus suggests to Jem whilst he was playing with his air rifle,

> I'd rather you shot at tin cans in the back yard, but I know you'll go after birds. Shoot all the bluejays you want, if you can hit 'em, but remember it's a sin to kill a mocking bird.

It was obvious Scout had not understood Atticus' message because she asked Miss Maudie Atkinson about it and even then she only had a superficial understanding of it. At this stage in the novel Scout was not aware of the more complex issues that could be associated with such a stricture.

Throughout the novel Scout learns about basic unfairness of the world and, due to her gaining more understanding of what Atticus had said, she realized something very important. After Tom's murder, Mr Underwood wrote a newspaper article and, after some thought, Scout understood how unfairly Tom Robinson was treated.

> Then Mr Underwood's meaning became clear.
> Atticus had used every tool available to free men to save Tom Robinson, but in the secret courts of men's hearts Atticus had no case. Tom was a dead man the minute Mayella Ewell opened her mouth and screamed.

The reason Scout had such clear comprehension was because of the reference in Mr Underwood's article of 'Tom's death to the senseless slaughter of songbirds'. She knew then that Tom just like the mocking bird, had committed no crime; from this she realizes that a black man, such as Tom Robinson, had no chance of a fair trial in front of a white jury. People could get away with condemning innocent black people the way people could frequently shoot the songbirds with no justification.

Finally, Scout's acquisition is highlighted because she now understands what Atticus said to Tom earlier in the novel about the mocking birds. It is clear that Boo Radley was the person who had bullied Bob Ewell with the knife. Mr Tate, who was in the Finch's home after this incident knew this and after a while so did Atticus, although at first he did think it was Tom. Scout's response to how Atticus explains what they must say about what happened, shows her complete understanding of what happened. It does not directly say but it is clear she realizes that it is Boo. 'Well it'd be sort of like shootin' a mocking bird, wouldn't it?' Scout realizes that, like the songbirds, Boo has done nothing to hurt anyone and he doesn't deserve to be punished.

Scout and Cassie both gain knowledge as each novel progresses. Even though they are both subject to difficulties as they learn, Cassie's life and the lesson she has to learn are much more harsh. Things that were painful for Scout, such as when people called her father 'nigger lover', a phrase she did not understand and when Bob Ewell spat in her father's face and threatened him, were devastating to Scout and to the life she led. Although compared to the situations Cassie was faced with they seemed far less brutal. Cassie had to accept white people were always going to be prejudiced towards her, although as a child she had not faltered. She had to face realities such as the burning of Mr Berry and the nightly attacks. Finally at the end of the novel she was a witness to the brutal, vicious and, most importantly, the unfair treatment of the Avery family. She had to watch whilst a boy who she had grown up with and his family were physically dragged out of their home and they were all severely beaten. Shocking scenes such as these would be very difficult for us to watch, least of all for a child who was also a friend of the people. After this ordeal, she was having to deal with the fact that T.J. who had strayed once as many children do, was going to be sentenced to death because of it. She had 'never liked T.J. but he had always been there'. At the end of the novel she did not understand what happened to T.J., she only saw it as wrong. This situation devastated Cassie, she 'cried for T.J.'.

Although in each novel there are very clear similarities there are also prominent differences. *Roll of Thunder Hear My Cry* is written from a black girl's perspective and *To Kill a Mocking Bird* is written from a white girl's view. Both novels are sympathetic to the black culture, although *Roll of Thunder Hear My Cry* gives a more positive view of black families. It shows the Logans to be very independent and also the novel has an educated black person, Maria Logan. *To Kill a Mocking Bird* shows the black people to be incredibly vulnerable. In Maycombe, the town where the novel is set, the black community is situated near to the town rubbish dump. *To Kill a Mocking Bird*, however, gives a true insight into the black culture and shows a positive side of the black people as well. Calpurnia and Mama Logan had been educated. When Scout and Jem accompanied Calpurnia to the black church, Scout, as a child, was incredibly impressed with the music and the language within the church. She received it for exactly what it was, a thriving culture, because she held no prejudices against black people.

Roll of Thunder Hear My Cry contains one main theory throughout the novel. It explains to the reader about the prejudice towards black families. Although *To Kill a Mocking Bird* covers this theme it also deals with Scout's process of growing up as a white girl. *Roll of Thunder Hear My Cry* describes Cassie's life as she is growing up but it also focuses on a central theme of prejudice; this enables the author to give a very graphic indication of what life was like in the 1930s.

To Kill a Mocking Bird in some ways seems to shield the reader from the harsh realities of life in the 1930s. This is probably because it is written from a white perspective and the prejudice is not the focal theme within the novel. Thus, Scout is not always influenced unlike Cassie because she is not subjected to direct prejudice.

Roll of Thunder Hear My Cry in some respects seems more realistic than *To Kill a Mocking Bird*, probably as it gives a harsh and less humorous view of life. The final part of the story brings the novel to an unhappy ending. This is unlike the ending of *To Kill a Mocking Bird* where the Finch family are close together and they have resumed back their normal, happy lives.

The one main issue in *Roll of Thunder Hear My Cry* results in Cassie throughout the novel experiencing and therefore learning most things about prejudice against black people. She learns that because she is black many people will treat her as inferior, a fact which will affect her for the rest of her life.

Unlike *Roll of Thunder Hear My Cry*, *To Kill a Mocking Bird* uses humour. Scout is a very funny character, her 'matter of fact' outlook onto life makes this novel much 'lighter' to read. The use of humour in *Roll of Thunder Hear My Cry* would not be suitable as the narrator is a victim of racial prejudice, the novel has a much more serious tone.

Both novels are very well written and extremely enjoyable to read.

ENGLISH: WORKED EXAMPLES

Response to Unseen Texts

Read the short story and the poem and answer all the questions that follow. You should spend about 45 minutes on this section.

Most of us have especially vivid memories of the place in which we grew up.

Jean Rhys was born and brought up on the West Indian island of Dominica but she spent most of her adult life travelling and working in Europe. The story was written after a return visit to her birthplace in the 1930s.

I USED TO LIVE HERE ONCE

*She was standing by the river looking at the stepping stones
and remembering each one. There was the round unsteady stone,
the pointed one, the flat one in the middle—the safe stone
where you could stand and look around. The next wasn't so safe
for when the river was full the water flowed over it and even
when it showed dry it was slippery. But after that it was easy
and soon she was standing on the other side.*

*The road was much wider than it used to be but the work had
been done carelessly. The felled trees had not been cleared
away and the bushes looked trampled. Yet it was the same road
and she walked along feeling extraordinarily happy.*

*It was a fine day, a blue day. The only thing was that the sky
had a glassy look that she didn't remember. That was the only
word she could think of. Glassy. She turned the corner, saw that
what had been the old pavement had been taken up, and there too the
road was much wider, but it had the same unfinished look.*

*She came to the worn stones that led up to the house and her
heart began to beat. The screw pine was gone, so was the mock
summer house called the ajoupa, but the clove tree was still
there and at the top of the steps the rough lawn stretched
away, just as she had remembered it. She stopped and looked
toward the house that had been added to and painted white. It
was strange to see a car standing in front of it.*

*There were two children under the big mango tree, a boy and a
little girl, and she waved to them and called 'Hello' but they
didn't answer her or turn their heads. Very fair children, as
Europeans born in the West Indies so often are: as if the white
blood is asserting itself against all odds.*

*The grass was yellow in the hot sunlight as she walked
towards them. When she was quite close she called again, shyly:
'Hello'. Then, 'I used to live here once,' she said.
Still they didn't answer. When she said for the third time
'Hello' she was quite near them. Her arms went out instinctively
with the longing to touch them.*

*It was the boy who turned, his grey eyes looked straight into
hers. His expression didn't change. He said, 'Hasn't it gone
cold all of a sudden. D'you notice? Let's go in.' 'Yes
let's', said the girl.*

*Her arms fell to her side as she watched them running across
the grass to the house. That was the first time she knew.*

John Betjeman spent much of his boyhood on The Greenaway, a small stretch of land on the north coast of Cornwall, and he used to return there regularly throughout his life.

GREENAWAY

I know so well this turfy mile,
    These clumps of sea-pink withered brown,
The breezy cliff, the awkward stile,
    The sandy path that takes me down.

To crackling layers of broken slate
    Where black and flat sea-woodlice crawl
And isolated rock pools wait
    The wash from the highest tides of all.

I know the roughly blasted track
    That skirts a small and smelly bay
And over squelching bladder-wrack
    Leads to the beach at Greenaway.

Down on the shingle safe at last
    I hear the slowly dragging roar
As mighty rollers mount to cast
    Small coal and seaweed on the shore.

And spurting far as it can reach
    The shooting surf comes hissing round
To leave a line along the beach
    Of cowries waiting to be found.

Tide after tide by night and day
    The breakers battle with the land
And rounded smooth along the bay
    The faithful rocks protecting stand.

But in a dream the other night,
    I saw this coastline from the sea
And felt the breakers plunging white
    Their weight of waters over me.

There were the stile, the turf, the shore,
    The safety line of shingle beach;
With every stroke I struck the more
    The backwash sucked me out of reach.

Back into what a water-world
    Of waving weed and waiting claws?
Of writhing tentacles uncurled
    To drag me to what dreadful jaws?

1. Examine the ways both authors use particular details to suggest their familiarity with the scenes they describe.

2. Do you think there is anything unusual or surprising about the endings of the two pieces? What do you think the authors are trying to suggest by treating their subject in this way?

In your answer you should refer to particular details to support your comment.

The unseen text is reproduced above. A start is made on answering the questions with a preliminary mapping.

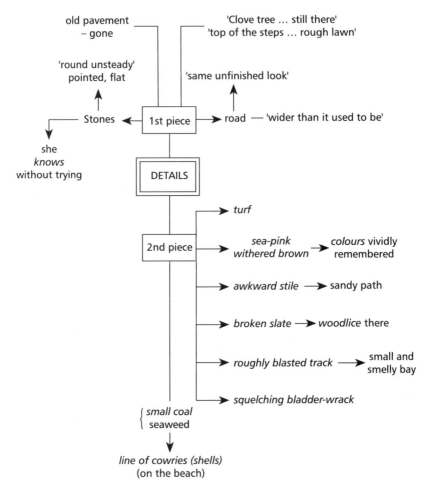

Mapping of Question 1

Further exercises

TASK

> Your school is taking part in a local Health Awareness campaign. Write a leaflet to be given out at the next Parent's meeting. Your leaflet should be directed at one of your parents or guardians and should aim to persuade them to become fit. Give the readers reasons why they should become fit; ways of making time; sports or pastimes that would suit them specifically. Try to predict any arguments that they might have against exercise.
>
> You may use the information on the next sheet if you wish, but do not simply copy it. You may also add ideas of your own.

INSTRUCTIONS

1. **Read the information** carefully. Make a note of the key points that you may wish to use in your leaflet.

2. **Plan your leaflet**. It should be organised and written for an adult. Think about who is going to read your leaflet and the best organisation to use. Write your plan in your answer book. (Spend about 10 minutes on this.)

3. **Write your leaflet**. Use your plan as a basis. Make sure that your language and layout are suitable for a leaflet to an adult. Take care with handwriting, presentation, spelling, and grammar.

4. **Check your leaflet**. At the end, check your leaflet carefully. Correct the spelling, grammar and punctuation to make it as accurate as you can. (Spend about 10 minutes on this).

Fit for what?

People talk about "being fit" ... but fit for what? You don't have to be an athlete to be fit. Your fitness level should be in tune with your lifestyle. You should have plenty of energy to climb stairs or take a brisk walk, as well as performing other day to day activities without becoming tired or gasping for breath.

Being fit not only makes you look and feel better, it has many pay-offs for your health. It strengthens your heart and improves your circulation. It can also help lower your blood pressure and blood cholesterol levels, control your weight and reduce your stress levels, all of which reduce your risk of suffering from serious illnesses such as heart disease.

How can I get fit?

All round fitness should include the three 's' factors. First, *stamina* which helps keep your heart and lungs healthy, muscular *strength* and *'stretchability'* to keep you supple and mobile. If you want to be collecting your old age pension in a tracksuit and training shoes, the time to start is today.

Exercise

All exercise is good for your body, but the best exercises for your heart are exercises which build your stamina. Stamina building exercise is any exercise where you exert yourself continuously over a period of time. This could be a brisk walk or jog, swimming or cycling at a good pace or an aerobic workout.

A good session of any type of exercise releases pent-up tension. It can be difficult at the end of a long day – but instead of slumping in front of the telly, try a brisk walk, or a swim. You'll be surprised how recharged you feel, how much extra energy you've gained.

The golden rules of exercise are to start gently, to build gradually, and to do it regularly! To be effective, most experts recommend two to three sessions per week of at least 20 minutes each time. Varying your activity helps keep you motivated and makes exercise more fun; so why not look in at your local sports centre or fitness club. Staff there are trained to help you develop a fitness programme which will suit your ability.

Sport

"I'd love to try a new sport, but I don't have the time"

It's a common complaint and there's only one solution – make time. You should aim to make exercise an enjoyable 'habit' so that it becomes a regular part of your life – just like cleaning your teeth. You'll soon find yourself with new-found energy which will enable you to achieve things more quickly and efficiently – in effect making more time for yourself. Joining a class or taking up a sport with a friend means you can encourage each other and adds extra enjoyment.

Activities you may not have considered like golf, sailing, windsurfing, tennis, pony trekking, canoeing, bowls and archery are available all over the country. The Sports Council (address overleaf) can give you more details about any new sport you would like to get involved with. Or if these sound too exotic perhaps you should think about activities, like walking, swimming or cycling, in a new light.

There's something for all the family, whatever age, or stage of fitness.

Tips about exercise & a caution

1. Try to sneak some exercise into your daily routine. Why not get off the bus a few stops early and walk the rest? Use the stairs instead of the lift and for short trips leave the car in the garage and enjoy the stroll.
2. Remember to start slowly and build gradually.
3. Exercise until pleasantly tired, but don't push to exhaustion. The right level will leave you breathless but not speechless.
4. Always warm-up to prepare your muscles before exercising and include some gentle stretches.

5. 'Wind down' your exercise session, don't stop suddenly following vigorous exercise. Slow the pace of your activity to a comfortable level for a few minutes at the end of your session.
6. Leave an hour after heavy meals before starting exercise.
7. Don't ignore pain – it's your body saying "stop!"
8. Easy, rhythmic movements are best – cycling, swimming and walking are the best all round forms of exercise.

BUT: You can start exercising at any time of life, but if you've not taken any exercise for some time, are over 40, have recently been ill or have any joint problems, check with your family doctor before doing anything too strenuous.

Billy Fisher lives in world of his own, where he can get away from his problems and the effects of his lies.

Write your own story where you keep drifting off into your own little worlds in order to escape your relatives, teachers and problems.

*L*YING *in bed, I abandoned the facts again and was back in Ambrosia.*

By rights, the march-past started in the Avenue of the Presidents, but it was an easy thing to shift the whole thing into Town Square. My friends had vantage seats on the town-hall steps where no flag flew more proudly than the tattered blue star of the Ambrosian Federation, the standard we had carried into battle. One by one the regiments marched past, and when they had gone — the Guards, the Parachutte Regiment, the King's Own Yorkshire Light Infantry — a hush fell over the crowds and they removed their hats for the proud remnants of the Ambrosian Grand Yeomanry. It was true that we had entered the war late, and some criticized us for that; but out of two thousand who went into battle only seven remained to hear the rebuke. We limped along as we had arrived from the battle-field, the mud still on our shredded uniforms, but with a proud swing to our kilts. The band played 'March of the Movies'. The war memorial was decked with blue poppies, the strange bloom found only in Ambrosia.

My mother shouted up the stairs: 'Billy? **Are** *you getting up?' the third call in a fairly well-established series of street-cries that graduated from: 'Are you awake, Billy?' to 'It's a quarter past nine, and you can stay in bed all day for all I care', meaning twenty to nine and time to get up. I waited until she called: 'If I come up there you'll* **know** *about it' (a variant of number five, usually 'If I come up there I shall* **tip** *you out') and then I got up.*

The following is a powerful description of someone on her own who imagines she is being followed. She frequently appeals to God whom she feels will protect her.

Write the story of yourself in a similar situation where you are being followed home from a late night out.

Note Bradbury's use of sentence length, images and paragraphing for effect. Try to utilise these effects in your work.

She ran across the bridge.

Oh God, God, please, please let me get up the hill! Now up the path, now between the hills, oh God, it's dark, and everything so far away. If I screamed now it wouldn't help; I can't scream anyway. Here's the top of the path, here's the street, oh, God, please let me be safe, if I get home safe I'll never go out alone; I was a fool, let me admit it, I was a fool. I didn't know what terror was, but if you let me get home from this I'll never go without Helen or Francine again! Here's the street. Across the street!

She crossed the street and rushed up the sidewalk.

Oh God, the porch! My house! Oh God, please give me time to get inside and lock the door and I'll be safe!

And there, silly thing to notice—why did she notice, instantly, no time, no time—but there it was anyway, flashing by—there on the porch rail, the half-filled glass of lemonade she had abandoned a long time, a year, half an evening ago! The lemonade glass sitting calmly, imperturbably there on the rail . . . and . . .

She heard her clumsy feet on the porch and listened and felt her hands scrabbling and ripping at the lock with the key. She heard her heart. She heard her inner voice screaming.

The key fit.

Unlock the door, quick, quick!

The door opened.

Now, inside, Slam it!

She slammed the door.

'Now lock it, bar it, lock it!' she gasped wretchedly.

*'Lock it, tight, **tight**!'*

Images of War

What attitudes to war have you found in the people about whom you have been reading, and how has the writer (or writers) helped you to share and understand the various experiences which those people have in war or conflict? Refer to details of the text(s) in your answer. Name your text(s) in your answer book.

You should include some or all of the following in your discussion:

- disturbing and moving experiences
- excitement and drama
- the writer's or writers' use of language.

Heroines and Heroes

Choose TWO characters who have impressed you by their ability to endure difficulties and troubles. Name the text(s) you are writing about in your answer book.

Write about the way they are changed by circumstances and about the way in which the writer presents these changes in order to make the circumstances vivid and memorable.

You should write about:

- how they endure the circumstances
- how they are changed
- how the changes are presented by the writer.

The Experience of School

Use any text you have read on this Area of Study. Name your text in your answer book.

Write about the views or impressions of school or education which the author conveys in the text.

You should write about:

- what the author conveys about school or education
- the language used
- the author's views on school and education
- how these views are presented.

Barry Hines: *A Kestrel for a Knave*

(a) Compare and contrast the three teachers in the novel (Mr Farthing, Mr Sugden and the headmaster, Mr Gryce).

(b) Explore what opinion you think the author wishes the reader to form of Billy's experience of school and how he reveals this opinion.

George Orwell: *Animal Farm*

1. "Man is the only real enemy we have," said Old Major. Who or what are the real enemies shown to us by the author in *Animal Farm* in your opinion, and how are they shown?

2.

Re-read the extract printed below and answer the following questions.

(a) What are the ways in which Napoleon is using Snowball and stories about him to his own advantage in this extract?

(b) What details show Napoleon's increasing power and authority in this section?

(c) Examine Squealer's speech in lines 54 - 63. What are the ways in which Squealer tries to convince his audience? How does he do it?

(d) Explain how Orwell treats the idea of rewriting history. Use both this extract and the novel as a whole for your answer.

One Sunday morning Squealer announced that the hens, who had just come in to lay again, must surrender their eggs. Napoleon had accepted, through Whymper, a contract for four hundred eggs a week. The price of these would pay for enough grain and meal to keep the farm going till summer came on and conditions were easier.

5   When the hens heard this, they raised a terrible outcry. They had been warned earlier that this sacrifice might be necessary, but had not believed that it would really happen. They were just getting their clutches ready for the spring sitting, and they protested that to take the eggs away now was murder. For the first time since the expulsion of Jones there was something resembling a rebellion. Led by three young Black Minorca pullets,

10 the hens made a determined effort to thwart Napoleon's wishes. Their method was to fly up to the rafters and there lay their eggs, which smashed to pieces on the floor. Napoleon acted swiftly and ruthlessly. He ordered the hens' rations to be stopped, and decreed that any animal giving so much as a grain of corn to a hen should be punished by death. The dogs saw to it that these orders were carried out. For five days the hens held out,

15 then they capitulated and went back to their nesting boxes. Nine hens had died in the meantime. Their bodies were buried in the orchard, and it was given out that they had died of coccidiosis. Whymper heard nothing of this affair, and the eggs were duly delivered, a grocer's van driving up to the farm once a week to take them away.

  All this while no more had been seen of Snowball. He was rumoured to be hiding on

20 one of the neighbouring farms, either Foxwood or Pinchfield. Napoleon was by this time on slightly better terms with the other farmers than before. It happened that there was in the yard a pile of timber which had been stacked there ten years earlier when a beech spinney was cleared. It was well seasoned, and Whymper had advised Napoleon to sell it; both Mr. Pilkington and Mr. Frederick were anxious to buy it. Napoleon was hesitating

25 between the two, unable to make up his mind. It was noticed that whenever he seemed on the point of coming to an agreement with Frederick, Snowball was declared to be hiding at Foxwood, while, when he inclined towards Pilkington, Snowball was said to be at Pinchfield.

  Suddenly, early in the spring, an alarming thing was discovered. Snowball was secretly

30 frequenting the farm by night! The animals were so disturbed that they could hardly sleep in their stalls. Every night, it was said, he came creeping in under cover of darkness and performed all kinds of mischief. He stole the corn, he upset the milk-pails, he broke the eggs, he trampled the seed-beds, he gnawed the bark off the fruit trees. Whenever anything went wrong it became usual to attribute it to Snowball. If a window was broken

35 or a drain blocked up, someone was certain to say that Snowball had come in the night and done it, and when the key of the store-shed was lost, the whole farm was convinced that Snowball had thrown it down the well. Curiously enough, they went on believing this even after the mislaid key was found under a sack of meal. The cows declared

unanimously that Snowball crept into their stalls and milked them in their sleep. The
40 rats, which had been troublesome that winter, were also said to be in league with Snowball.
   Napoleon decreed that there should be a full investigation into Snowball's activities.
With his dogs in attendance he set out and made a careful tour of inspection of the farm
buildings, the other animals following at a respectful distance. At every few steps Napoleon
stopped and snuffed the ground for traces of Snowball's footsteps, which, he said, he
45 could detect by the smell. He snuffed in every corner, in the barn, in the cowshed, in
the hen-houses, in the vegetable garden, and found traces of Snowball almost everywhere.
He would put his snout to the ground, give several deep sniffs, and exclaim in a terrible
voice, 'Snowball! He has been here! I can smell him distinctly!' and at the word 'Snowball'
all the dogs let out blood-curdling growls and showed their side teeth.
50   The animals were thoroughly frightened. It seemed to them as though Snowball were
some kind of invisible influence, pervading the air about them and menacing them with
all kinds of dangers. In the evening Squealer called them together, and with an alarmed
expression on his face told them that he had some serious news to report.
   'Comrades!' cried Squealer, making little nervous skips, 'a most terrible thing has been
55 discovered. Snowball has sold himself to Frederick of Pinchfield Farm, who is even now
plotting to attack us and take our farm away from us! Snowball is to act as his guide
when the attack begins. But there is worse than that. We had thought that Snowball's
rebellion was caused by his vanity and ambition. But we were wrong, comrades. Do
you know what the real reason was? Snowball was in league with Jones from the very
60 start! He was Jones's secret agent all the time. It has all been proved by documents which
he left behind him and which we have only just discovered. To my mind this explains
a great deal, comrades. Did we not see for ourselves how he attempted — fortunately
without success — to get us defeated and destroyed at the Battle of the Cowshed?'
   The animals were stupefied. This was a wickedness far outdoing Snowball's destruction
65 of the windmill. But it was some minutes before they could fully take it in.

six

GCSE languages

Learning a language can be easy if a few basic principles are followed. These are exactly the same rules that apply to learning in general.

For GCSE there is a set syllabus and for the National Curriculum this needs to be laid down in *themes* (e.g. Family, Food and Drink) so that each theme includes closely-related items (words, phonics, intonation). Each file will then be available for a *search-scan* at *recall*; time and practice, both verbal and theoretical, will reduce *search-and-find time*. Themes are mind-mapped for ease of scanning.

Once such a filing system has been organized, each individual item has to be translated into concrete picture form to link with something in memory. This includes not only the visual structure of a word, for example, but also its sound:

le livre has to correspond to
the book and is easily translated:
le ⟶ the (rhyme) ⟶ idiosyncratic (odd) image
        or   of *shape* of word
      male-book

90% rule helps: most feminine words end in 'e'
idiosyncratic image of word structure:

livres ⟶ *leaves* (of a book) ⟶ books

The trick is in creating a *sequence* of clear, concrete images which link the foreign word closely to the concrete image established in memory.

The example above, however, illustrates a *ready link* (a near-cognate). The pegging of the word *livre* is accomplished without recourse to an additional mnemonic. As with all learning, results are achieved much quicker if there is *conscious* formation of images and the link. Parrot-repetition of a word (old-fashioned drill) is a highly inefficient learning method because it is simply a method of attempting concentration on the word in order to create an image. Whether you learn will depend on whether your concentration is deep enough and image-provoking.

The difficulties encountered in learning a language are usually where links between experience in memory and the word or phrase are difficult to establish.

For example:

la fenêtre ⟶ . . .? . . . window

A link must be made, but there are no easy word links. In this case the common mental picture is the link:

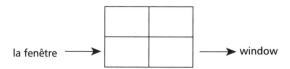

The circumflex ˆ is useful to create an idiosyncratic image where the word wraps itself round the top of the window-picture, like a *cap* or *hat*:

fenêtre

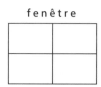

In French *la* and *le, un* and *une* can cause some difficulty for pupils until they realize that *le* or *la* must always be learnt in association with the word. Alternatively, or in concert, you can attach the image of a man or woman to every object and remember them in this way.

la fenêtre

(This supplements the 90% rule in French.)

STORY-TELLING WITHIN A THEME

Story-telling is most effective in two situations:

1 You are on your own; you need to learn a number of words and phrases, so you *imagine* yourself as, for example, a customer in a shop buying from a shopkeeper. You have to *create* his questions and your answers. You *speak* the words out loud *and* write them down. Listening to a tape of a similar situation also creates the situation in your mind. Many language learning systems on disc and tape use this method.
2 You take the *role* of shopkeeper or customer and enact a scene.

It is invaluable to have a mind map of words and phrases which can be used in the situation. Words are best learnt if they have pictures appended.

SENTENCE SYNTHESIS

Although the knowledge of *word-meanings* is at the heart of learning a language (a person in a foreign country can manage by pointing and the use of basic words), the construction of sentences extends knowledge dramatically. For GCSE, practice *within* a theme using the following words can develop *twenty-five* simple statements:

voici	une plume
voilà	un cahier
Je vois	un crayon
Il a	un livre
Nous avons	un pupitre

Many pupils lack knowledge of prepositions, and the same system can build up more combinations into simple sentences:

Derrière	Jean	il y a	un avion
Devant	l'auto	nous voyons	mon grand-père
Au-dessous de	la maison	Pierre voit	un petit enfant
Au-dessous de	l'arbre	se trouvre	un phantôme
A côté de	nos amis	Marie dessine	

Adverb phrases extend the range of further sentences (and lead to higher grading):

je	sortir	l'église	à toute allure
Il	entrer dans	la tour carrée	sans mot dire
Solange et moi	passer devant	la boutique	à leur insu

The following relates particularly to French for GCSE, but the principles are applicable for any language. See mind-map 1 on the next page.

Literal translation is often an effective link between the written language and English:

à ce moment-là
at that moment there

is idiosyncratic and *memorable* because in literal translation, it seems to be repetitious. The real meaning links easily to the image of someone pointing feverishly at a point in time.

So-called 'notions' (i.e. conceptual phrases) are full of such image-provoking groups of words:

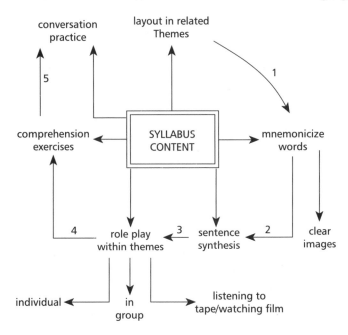

Language mind-map 1

Combien de temps?
Combine the temps?
How much of time?
How long?

Quel âge avez-vous?
What age have you?
How old are you?

il n'y a pas
He there has not
He isn't there
There isn't

y-a-t-il?
there has he?
is there?

Once the link has been made between the image associated with the English words and the original French, practice will *seal* this link. The *interesting images* will eventually dim through lack of use.

STRATEGIES FOR LEARNING

Reading and understanding is different from *listening* and understanding and, although in GCSE these skills tend to be separated, French word and sound and English word and sound should be learnt together. This is because *recall* is easier according to the greater the number of closely-associated images:

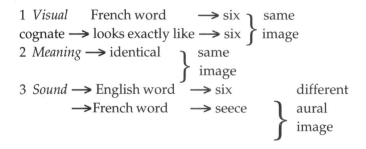

1 *Visual*   French word   → six ⎫ same
cognate → looks exactly like → six ⎬ image
2 *Meaning* → identical ⎫ same
⎬ image
3 *Sound* → English word → six   different
→French word → seece ⎫ aural
⎬ image

There is an additional, reinforcing image link: counting in French is easily learnt because we already have a very well-used, rhythmic succession of corresponding images in English:

one two three four five six . . .
un deux trois quatre cinq six . . .

Aids to visualizing

Because visualizing is the key to effective memorization, and the *clearer* the mental picture you can produce, the better remembered is the word or phrase, a 3-D mnemonic is one of the most effective known. It

involves building up a phrase by substituting different coloured rods
(or pencils) for each individual word. The rod (pencil) is the intermediate between the words. For example:

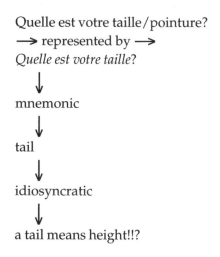

Quelle est votre taille/pointure?
⟶ represented by ⟶
Quelle est votre taille?

↓

mnemonic

↓

tail

↓

idiosyncratic

↓

a tail means height!!?

Links for phrase

How is your height?
(to fix sentence structure in French)

↓

How tall are you?

Point to each rod (pencil) in order (or any order) and visualize phrase
and word in place of the pencil. This system can be extended to memorize texts of much greater length. As you learn the text:

You are learning the *words*
You are learning *phrases*
You are learning how to *write* in French

You can enact dialogue using the rods (cuisenaire rods, for counting, as
used in primary schools are very effective in this exercise) within
themes and in general (theme-linking) discussions.

A rod is not an intermediate in learning – it is not a true mental link. It is a form of 'background' on which rehearsal can be effected, facilitating concentration to produce the image. Coloured rods on a *clear* table-top as background greatly enhance the effectiveness. Furthermore, many students take a few rods (or pencils) into examinations to aid them!

MIND-MAPS

The fifteen themes for languages that follow can be used equally for any language. There follows a dissection of the first theme into sub-themes, each of which you should work within to develop word knowledge, phrasing, grammar, conversation and listening skills and writing. The aim, at some point along a branch of a map, is to indicate the *meaning* of the word or phrase. Meaning does not always have to be *spelt* out, but where a word is difficult to remember a mnemonic should be added.

Strategies for understanding text in original form

For the Higher Level, text will be presented containing words that you may not have seen before. For example:

Il s'est assis sous une mancienne: dans ses branches un oiseau chantait.

'Mancienne' can be inferred to be some sort of tree because someone is sitting beneath it, and in its branches sings a bird.

Certain patterns of word formation can lead you to the meaning of words, as can be seen in the mind-map that follows.

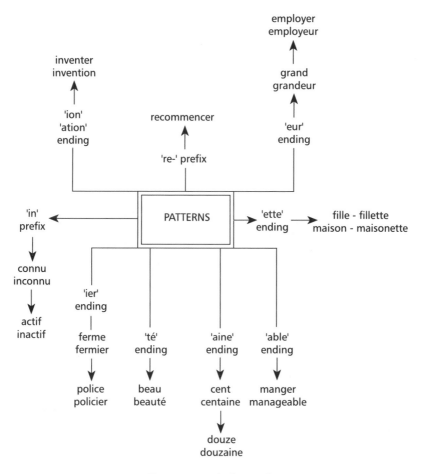

Language mind-map 2

Strategies for reading and understanding text with the set vocabulary

Apart from *cognates* (same visual form, same meaning) like innocents, justice, muscle, rectangle, and *near-cognates* which have *nearly* the same form, there are common patterns between French and English:

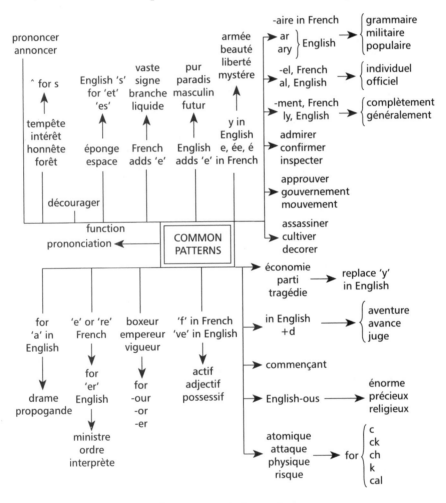

Language mind-map 3

Theme areas

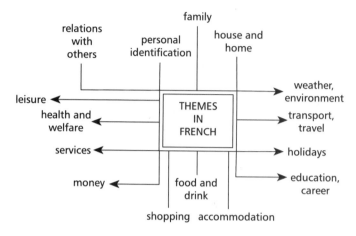

Language mind-map 4

Each theme area can be sub-divided into small topic areas within which files of vocabulary can be created and used for writing, listening and speaking. A typical split into topic areas is in the personal area.

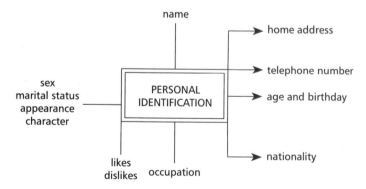

Language mind-map 5

The *Name* file can be created as follows:

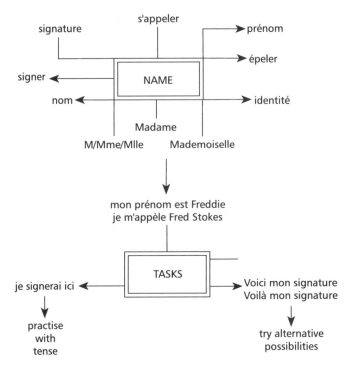

Language mind-map 6

When all possible images have been created within this file area (including mnemonics pegging word *shapes*, *sounds* or meanings), a closely related file can be created, e.g. home address. Establish links between files by tacking new phrases / sentences onto those already created. When the complete *personal* set of files is complete, a new set of, say, *family* files can be created by an easy bridge.

Identification is quite an extensive theme and will require several maps, to include Higher Level words and expressions. *Money* is a smaller theme, however, and can be incorporated into a single mind-map.

All words and phrases should be included on a mind-map, but the structure of the file should not become overloaded. Several maps per theme is perfectly acceptable and, in fact, nearly always necessary.

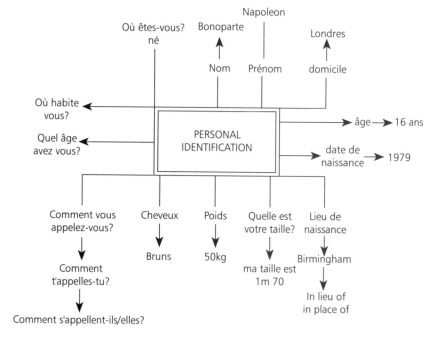

Language mind-map 7

LANGUAGE EXERCISES

In the following examples, answers should be in English.

6 Next you look at the TV page of the booklet.

PROGRAMMES DE TÉLÉVISION

CANAL 01 - Informations Hôtel

CANAL 02 - Radio France Musique

CANAL 03 - TF 1

CANAL 04 - A 2

CANAL 05 - FR 3

CANAL 06 - CANAL +

Touche marche/arrêt sur la télécommande

Possibilité de louer un magnétoscope sur demande.
Veuillez vous adresser à la réception.

What does it say in the last two lines at the bottom of the page?

....

.... *(2)*

7 The following day you decide to explore the town on foot. First you go to a "Maison des Jeunes" to get some leaflets. This is the first one you pick up.

POUR LIRE, TELEPHONEZ

ALLO BIBLIO

Club.

Envie de lire, besoin d'un livre, mais...
pas le temps de chercher, pas le temps de vous
déplacer,... la solution?

ALLO BIBLIO CLUB

Commandez vos livres par téléphone,
nous vous les expédions rapidement.

**24 HEURES SUR 24
7 JOURS SUR 7**

What is it about?

....

....

....

.... *(2)*

While travelling back home at the end of your holiday you read this letter in 'Phosphore' magazine.

COURRIER
LES ADULTES NE NOUS ÉCOUTENT PAS

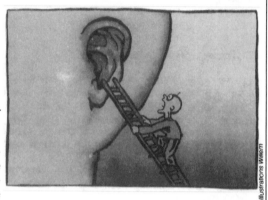

Illustrations Willem

Je voudrais répondre à Marie (*Phosphore*, n° 109-février.) qui se sent méprisée.

Ta lettre Marie, m'a beaucoup intéressée car je ressens souvent la même chose que toi... Tu dis que ton problème n'en est pas un, mais moi je pense le contraire... Il est très important car je crois qu'il concerne tous les jeunes d'aujourd'hui. Toi, tu es une personne à part entière qui a le droit de s'exprimer comme tout le monde. Les adultes ont tendance à penser que nous les jeunes, nous ne savons pas de quoi nous parlons et que nous sommes incapables d'avoir des idées précises, il nous sous-estiment! Alors ils nous laissent de côté en nous répétant de nous taire car nous n'y connaissons rien... Eh bien moi je dis non! Je crois que la société doit nous écouter, car nous avons des choses à dire! Je ne dis pas que toutes nos idées sont justes, mais que c'est par la confrontation avec les adultes que nos pensées pourront évoluer et s'épanouir. Il y a des adultes qui « se la jouent » un peu trop et qui feraient mieux d'écouter ce que pensent les jeunes... Je suis sûre qu'ils pourraient apprendre beaucoup. Car nous voyons les choses d'une autre manière et cela peut toujours apporter des éléments de réponse à certains problèmes.

Cécile, 1re S.

What main points does Cécile make in her letter?

....

....

....

....

....

....

....

....

Your neighbours ask you to help them with this letter they have received from a French camp site.

CAMPING "LES ROCHES"
CAROUAL - VILLAGE
22430 ERQUY - Tél. 96 72 32 90
EURL au Capital de 50.000 F.
Siret 353 786 452 00014

Le 18/6

Madame, Monsieur,

Nous avons bien reçu votre chèque de 155,00F et vous en remercions.

Nous vous confirmons donc votre réservation d'un emplacement du 8 au 16 Août prochain.

A bientôt!

M. Barbedienne

What does the letter say?

....

....

(2)

seven

Other subjects at GCSE

The subjects dealt with in this chapter include geography, history, business studies, music and art and design.

Where facts, principles and problem-solving are concerned, the methods of learning already used in this book apply:

a Theme the information. (In history, dated events theme effectively for ease of learning, e.g. the American Civil War.)
b Map the themed information and/or principles.
c 'Peg' the theme and mnemonicize, diagram and story-link the thematic information.

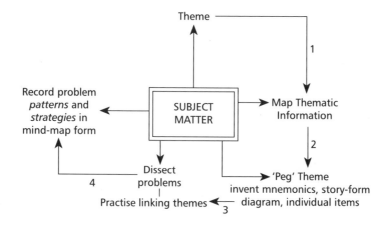

d Practise dissecting problems and thus linking information using mind maps.

e Spot *patterns* and employ *strategies* in exam questions, and map them also.

The following is a general treatment of the skills necessary for the various subjects. Sample material is included at the end of the chapter.

GEOGRAPHY

Skills you will need to learn involve:

- Fieldwork
- Mapping
- Graphs (line, bar, scatter)
- Diagrams
- Photographic interpretation
- Sketching

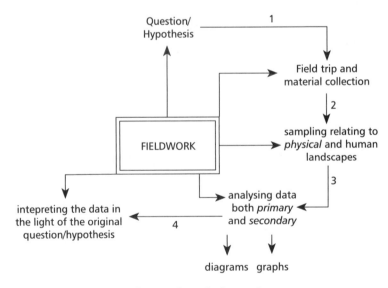

Geography mind-map 1

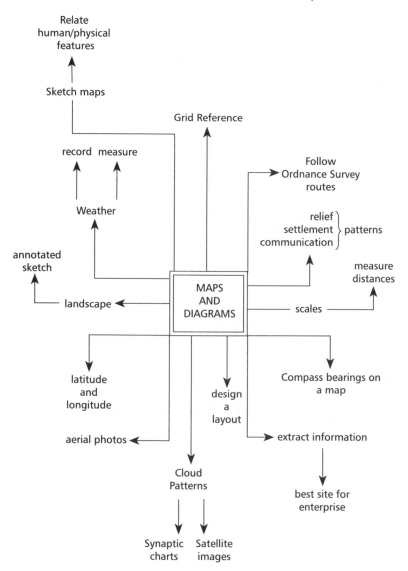

Geography mind-map 2

Fieldwork

Either you or your teacher will choose a topic (e.g. compare the effect of topography on the towns of Castleton and Hathersage). You will *either* be given a question to answer or a hypothesis to be tested.

There is a variety of aspects of maps and diagrams that you must be able to understand and have practice in; as can be seen in mind-map 2.

HISTORY

For history you need to identify primary sources (such as photos, drawings, diaries, letters, wills, statistics, etc. at the time of the event) and secondary sources (books or articles based on primary sources).

The teaching of history is in a state of flux at the present time and is the subject of some controversy. Whether or not the weight of testing will fall mostly on factual content or on interpretation, only time will tell. See history mind-map on the following page.

BUSINESS STUDIES

Business studies in GCSE is organized into five major theme areas, as shown in mind-map 1 on page 232.

The National Criteria for Business Studies is incorporated into GCSE and includes mostly business studies and an *option* (e.g. information technology, commerce, finance and accounting).

Business studies lends itself to diagramming, flow diagrams and mind-mapping. For example, for the production process, see mind-map 2 on page 232.

For distribution, see mind-map 3 on page 233.

And for marketing, see mind-map 4 on page 233.

Systems theory provides scope for extensive mind-mapping as can be seen in mind-map 5 on page 233.

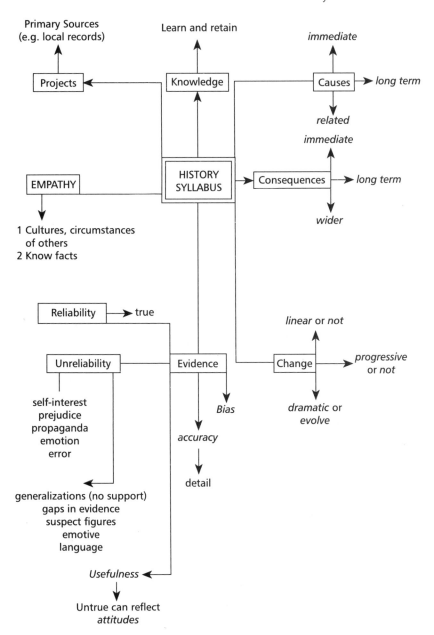

History mind-map

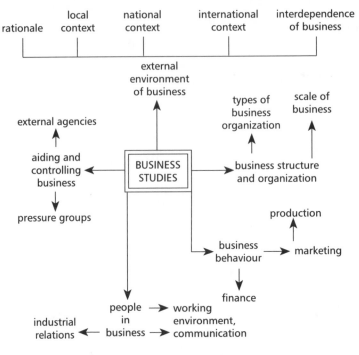

Business studies mind-map 1

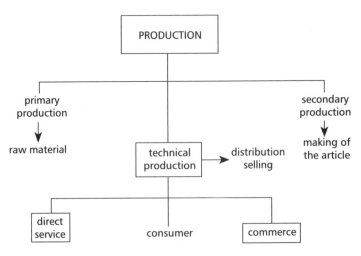

Business studies mind-map 2

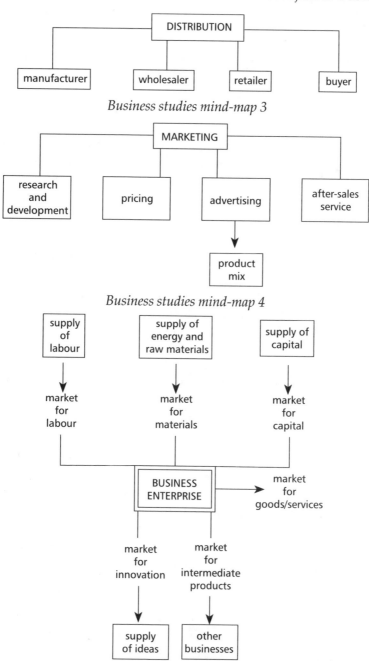

Business studies mind-map 3

Business studies mind-map 4

Business studies mind-map 5

MUSIC

As mentioned previously, in common with everything we learn, music too is memorized and, as such, needs to be visualized. Facts related to the GCSE syllabus can be mind-mapped and mnemonics applied to difficult words or concepts.

The learning of any instrument requires practice. As a musician myself (piano and clarinet) I have had to do my share of endless repetition of Chopin's overtures and Beethoven's sonatas. When later I played piano and organ for church services and meetings, work sometimes limited practice for specific pieces and then, without a piano to practise on, I would sit with a score on my knee on a bus or at a desk, mentally rehearsing both notation and timing. I found, on countless occasions, that this was more than equal to concrete 'hands-on' practice; although, with no practice at all, muscular co-ordination would have decreased. Invariably, also, I learnt the pieces by heart. The pages and the notes, in association with rhythm and tune, I could forever 'float' before my eyes at will.

Even when practising, it is important to develop deep concentration by attempting to visualize what you are playing. Perfect pitch, for example, is merely one aspect of memory – memorized pitch. Some have developed (memorized) perfect pitch at an early age and simply *build* on that when memorizing a major 3rd or minor triad. Music, rather like maths, is a 'building' block subject. This is most obvious in the manipulative department: five-finger exercises must be built upon two- and three-finger exercises for example. In the same way that some processes in maths, for example, tables, should be automatic (for everyday life, not just for GCSE), so correct fingering of scales in the octave position must be automatic before 3rds or 6ths can be safely tackled.

The 'building' is similar in theory of music. The understanding of intervals depends on the understanding of major scale structure and knowledge of major key signatures. The routes to these prerequisites must be readily accessible (well-worn paths) before more advanced concepts or procedures can be built on to them (linked). Elementary rules of learning apply even to aural ones because these *create images*, too. Different keys can be mind mapped and *pegged* by *mnemonics*, just as visual information can. The recognition of keys could be 'pegged', for example, by memorizing the first four bars of, say Beethoven's symphonies, recording these on tape and memorizing them in order. To 'peg' the key effectively you create an image (e.g. Pastoral, a golden-headed wheat field basking under an azure summer sky). When you are asked to determine the key of an unknown piece, you simply match the image of that key with each of your memorized mind-map keys. (The system works fast – so avoid 'snap' answers like, 'It's Beethoven's Fifth.')

Art and Design

Endorsed (specialized) course for art and design are: drawing and painting, graphics, textiles, 3D studies and photography. You will have chosen from one of these on the general course. To achieve top grades you will need to think divergently to provide varieties of solutions as well as different ways of reaching these solutions. The following are some suggestions for themes and materials that could be used for your artwork.

Other cultures:
Suggestions for research projects on a particular period or place:

Ancient Egypt	Indonesian
Aztec	Inuit
Benin	Islamic
Berber	Japan
Borneo	Masai
China	Medieval/Gothic
Classical Greece	Mongol
Classical Rome	Red Indian
Dogon	Turkish
Indian	Victorian

Suggested themes for design projects:

A publicity campaign: promoting our city	I protest!
	Packaging
Bedsitter	Record Sleeves
Car dashboards	Robots
Clothes	Shoes
Designing for the old and young	Seating
	Street style
Hats	Toys

Artists, art movements and art themes to study and adapt:

Abstract Art	Nude
Bauhaus	Portraiture
Bosch	Pre-Raphaelites
Cubists	Turner and the Romantics
David Hockney	Stanley Spencer
Impressionists	Still Life
Italian Renaissance	James Whistler
Kandinsky	Vermeer and the Dutch School
L. S. Lowry	

Suggestions for themes for your own artwork:

Carnival	Posters/Labels/Logos
Cartoonists	Puzzle
Celebrations	Reflections
Cities of the future	Rhythm
Clothes	Shadows
Comic characters	Shoes
Dragons and dinosaurs	Shops
Fear/horror	Splash
Friendship	Speed
Happiness	Star quality
Meeting	They're almost human
Nightlife	Under the sea
Noise	Weddings
Over the rainbow	Weekly self-portrait

To succeed in GCSE art you will need to develop your *visual perception* and *skills* associated with *investigating* and *making* in art, craft and design. You will also need to include the history of art, diverse artistic heritage and a variety of other artistic traditions. For this second strand it helps if you comb galleries, museums and art centres for ideas that you can extend – what if the artist had been interested in other shapes and colours, for example? You can also try to look at works of art from 'another point of view'. Not only is the image important but also our *feelings* when we view something. Your personal interpretation of some aspect of life makes for good art. In design, you must be aware of the sensibilities of others. Your work (e.g. a chair) must be both aesthetically pleasing and *user-friendly*.

The assessment of objectives for GCSE art and design are outlined in the mind-map below.

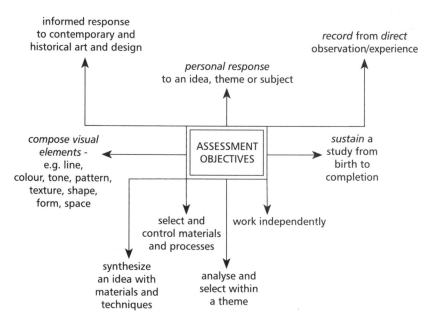

Art and design mind-map

eight

Examination revision and technique

In preparation for your revision, in whatever subject, all facts, principles and processes will need to be organized into theme areas. *Key words* and *key diagrams* can then be laid out in mind-map form, making sure that each map or 'file' contains only enough information to be absorbed in about two or three minutes. Sequential information (e.g. the plot of a book) is best arranged by starting from the '12 o'clock' position and ending at '11 o'clock'.

Any information that you find difficult to memorize should be made more concrete by devising mnemonics, whether using story form or linked facts, diagrams or letters. As you revise, you should make a conscious effort to visualize everything, including things like mathematical processes (e.g. how to multiply a matrix, transformations). For languages, learning is faster if you *rehearse* role play within a theme area and by *linking* themes (e.g. take yourself, in French, through breakfast conversation, out of the house and to the shops – all this in your head!) Not only the role play needs to be visualized, but also the individual words and phrases. This takes a certain amount of mental effort, but will have startling results.

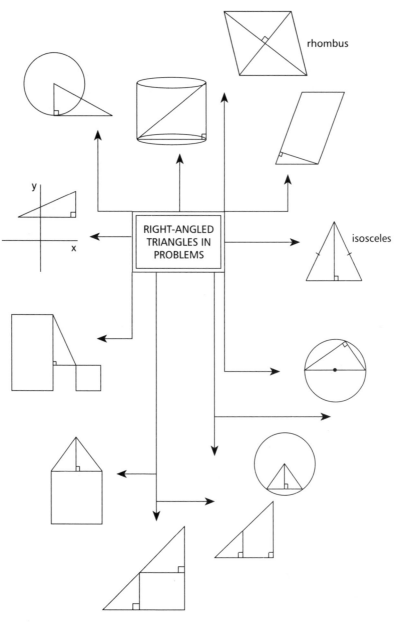

rhombus

isosceles

RIGHT-ANGLED TRIANGLES IN PROBLEMS

Maths revision mind-map

EXAM QUESTIONS AND PROBLEMS

You will also need to obtain past exam papers and syllabuses from the Exam Board. Straightforward questions will give you practice in recalling facts, principles and processes. Problems will develop your ability to *dissect* and *link* items of information to achieve a single answer, and also test your powers of *divergent* thinking.

Patterns in problems

One of the benefits of doing exam problems is that you will gradually begin to spot patterns and these can be organized into themes themselves. A *problem pattern* is a series of ways in which facts can be linked for testing. In trigonometry and Pythagoras questions, for example, right-angled triangles are half-submerged in a confusing picture. See mind-map on previous page.

Examiners frequently favour using a certain *pattern* or *form* of a question. When you spot this form recurring again and again in papers, it will help you to set it down on paper in the form of a *dissection web*:

Example Calculate the *reflex* angle between the hands of a clock at 6.45p.m.

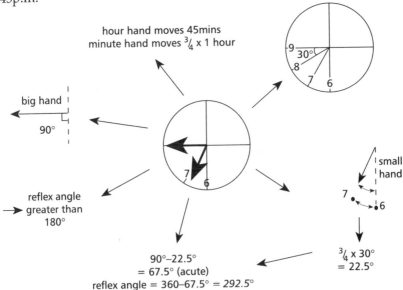

hour hand moves 45mins
minute hand moves ³/₄ x 1 hour

big hand
90°

reflex angle
greater than
180°

small
hand

90°–22.5°
= 67.5° (acute)
reflex angle = 360–67.5° = 292.5°

³/₄ x 30°
= 22.5°

The problem is more complex than it first looks. Dissecting it out into a web and setting it down, rather than merely doing the operations in your head, will commit it to long-term memory as a file of separate items of information. The web, however, is still only a *representation* of how you would work out the problem, because that is done by visualizing the rotation of hour and minute hands and comparing how far the hour hand moves when the minute hand moves through 270°. When revising this problem form you will need to *visualize* this rotation.

Brainstorming

You will also need to practise brainstorming for ideas in open-ended questions (common in English papers) or in divergent problems (e.g. in Science). Frequently, too, the maps you produce in revision time will be of use in the exam itself. In other words, the maps can be learnt in exactly the way that you learn from the syllabus mind-maps. They represent forms and patterns of *ordering facts* for particular questions. If you have files of such maps in long-term memory you start the exam with a distinct advantage – it could be said that you have *read* the mind of the examiner!

Divergent thinking problem   Suggest *two* advantages of generating electricity using *wave* energy instead of using *fossil* fuels.

Brainstorming (First see mind-maps over page)
Two advantages of using waves to produce electricity are:

1 There is no environmentally harmful waste.
2 Wave energy is renewable.

You will note that it does *not* detract from the exercise to consider the advantages of fossil fuels as well. In fact, it actually *helps* to consider *all* related facts because links in your long-term memory may not be exactly where you think they are. This is one reason for the 'tip-of-my-tongue- effect'. In searching through the files of your long-term memory sometimes you open the wrong files again and again, thinking

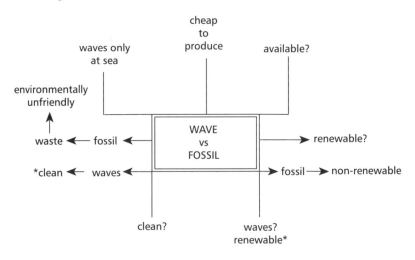

that the unrecalled fact is somewhere there. It isn't. It is in another file that you haven't yet looked through. Brainstorming frees your mind to search elsewhere, without being restrained by your conscious inhibitions. Using mnemonics as pegs ensures that you search immediately in the correct place, so if you feel there is any chance of forgetting something, *peg it* immediately using one of the methods already detailed in this book.

'KNOWING' AND 'THINKING YOU KNOW'

Sometimes candidates seem to work very hard for exams, enter the exam and fail miserably. They say, 'My mind went blank' or, 'I get exam nerves.'

The reason for exam nerves is always that a student does not have the information at his or her finger-tips. This is a problem of recall, it is not that the information is not *somewhere* in the long-term memory. Often the student has read and reread notes over and over again. The confusing images which the notes have created in the mind have scattered information indiscriminately throughout long-term memory. Without organized files and consciously creating mental pictures using mnemonics etc. recall is extremely difficult. A pressurizing question results in the mind's response of, 'Where on earth did I put *that* in long-term memory?' Effectively, then, exam revision should involve as much attention as possible to ensuring *maximum recall*.

When to revise

If your work is organized into a series of well-constructed mind-maps, these can be used for revision right up to the moment of the exam. This is in contrast to the last-minute use of notes, which will simply confuse the mind by creating *fuzzy* pictures and having searches initiated for matching information all over long-term memory. The mind-maps and associated mnemonics ensure that the lines to specifically useful information are open, so that recall is automatic. Furthermore, knowing that recall is going to be easy is conducive to a calm attitude and confidence.

EXAM TECHNIQUE

Good preparation is the key to success in exams. If facts, processes, principles and knowledge of the forms and patterns in *specific* subject exam problems are firmly embedded in long-term memory and are well *pegged* for recall, you will have little to worry about. But one word of warning: familiarity breeds contempt. Sometimes you can become so familiar with past exam questions and problems, that you fail to read them thoroughly when the actual exam time comes round. A quick scanning of a question will seem to identify a problem form or a pattern, and you launch into answering it. Examiners are well aware of such tendencies in students and will deliberately vary question form to 'catch' you out.

Sometimes students attempt a problem, trying to form a picture in their minds, and then give up. This is not good technique. As soon as you have read the question thoroughly, start jotting down the items in it and any processes that are relevant. The clear pictures you create on paper will make it easier for a match and links in long-term memory to be made.

Common errors

Apart from misreading the question, examiners identify many errors. Wandering off the point is a common mistake. It is a good idea to identify key words in a question, in English literature for example, and write it down on a piece of paper next to your answer paper. As you write, you can continually refer to it.

Bad planning of answers is another common error. Clumsy planning, or no planning, is immediately obvious. This can be overcome by setting down all relevant points in mind-map form before you start the question. The order of those points can also be mapped to achieve a well-constructed piece (use scrap paper for maps).

In the English-based subjects, also, *quality* is valued above quantity (this applies to assignments as well). You should aim for good presentation, including a check for spelling and punctuation; but be aware that excellent presentation without substance is instantly spottable. *Do not* use words whose meaning you are not absolutely sure of.

Some quotes from the text, in English for example, to support your reasoning are essential, and are often asked for in the question. However, *do not over-quote*. Basically, these are points that should have been well-learnt through assignment and exam practice work.

Concentration and thinking

Good preparation will make your passage through an exam far easier than it would otherwise have been; however, you are bound to find some aspect of GCSE that is fairly difficult. At this point, your competitive instinct should come to the surface and reinforce your concentration. The type of competitive thinking that you should muster is that type of thinking that will not admit defeat. This attitude breeds a string of A* results: it says 'I must know *everything* that faces me in an exam,' and even if this means leaving a problem until you have finished the rest of the paper, you should continue 'running through the finishing tape, as if in a running race'. One student I know, from a local comprehensive, wept unashamedly when she got 8 As and 2 Bs for her GCSE results; not because she was happy, but because she had missed a straight 10-A run! Perhaps this was a bit extreme, but at least it showed her determination. Another student worked extremely hard up to exam time, even working into the early hours of the night before the first exam. However, half-way through the exams, the impetus suddenly wore off and she eased down. The results showed the change in attitude: those for the first exams being excellent, but not so good for the later ones. Although I wouldn't advocate working to the late hours before exams, the effort must at least be consistent throughout exam time. With all you need for those exams laid out in easily digestible form, you can only gain from time spent scanning mind-maps.

CONCLUSION

This is a book that shows you how to learn and memorize; but not only that. It shows you *how* your mind works as you learn and memorize. Once you understand that, learning is no longer a mystery or a special skill. Learning rests firmly in your hands and, as far as academic success is concerned, it is possible to work out your own salvation. Good luck!

Other useful information

EXAMINATION BOARDS

You will need to order syllabuses and examination papers from the Boards setting your exams:

MEG   Midland Examining Group
           1 Hills Road
           Cambridge
           CB1 2EU

NEAB   Northern Examinations and Assessment Board
           Devas Street
           Manchester M15 6EX

NISEAC   Northern Ireland Examinations and Assessment council
           Beechhill House
           42 Beechhill Road
           Belfast
           BT8 4RS

SEB   Scottish Examining Board
           Ironmills Road
           Dalkeith
           Midlothian
           EH22 1LE

SEG   Southern Examining Group
               Stag Hill House
               Guildford
               GU2 5JX

ULEAC   University of London Examinations and Assessment
               Council
               Stewart House
               32 Russell Square
               London WC1B 5DN

WJEC   Welsh Joint Education Committee
               245 Western Avenue
               Cardiff
               CF5 2YX

BOOKS AND OTHER INFORMATION

Study books

There are study books on most GCSE subjects including:

Letts Study Guides
Longman Revise Guides

The Letts Study Guide for *Single and Double Award Science* is particularly well presented (diagrams, etc.).

For *English* good books include:
A New English Course (GCSE Edition) by Rhodri Jones (Macmillan).
New Dimensions (Collins English Programme) (Collins Educational).
Language Links by Jim Sweetman (Collins Educational).

English Literature Guides include *Lett's Explore* and *York Notes*.

With notes for GCSE on all main texts including:

Animal Farm
Lord of the Flies
Macbeth
Romeo and Juliet
An Inspector Calls

For *mathematics* excellent books are:
1 *Mathematics to Level 10* by Bostock and Chandler (Stanley Thornes)
2 *GCSE Maths 'Level A'* by Jean Holderness (Causeway Press Ltd, 1993).

For *French* look at *Auto Examen* (Collins Educational).

Dictionaries
English and foreign language dictionaries and foreign phrase books are available from the following publishers:

1 HarperCollins
2 Penguin
3 Oxford University Press (including the Oxford Mini reference)
4 Harrap's (including the Mini dictionary)

Tapes
1 BBC Enterprises: BBC Courses in General and for beginners.
2 Macmillan Educational.

Disks
For Amiga, PC:

1 ADI GCSE (Maths, English, French) from Europress.
2 *Mind-Map GCSE* from Future, Bridgeman Buildings, Bolton, Greater Manchester (Science, Maths).
3 *The BBC Shakespeare CD-ROM: Romeo and Juliet* (HarperCollins *Interactive*/BBC/Attica Cybernetics).
4 *The BBC Shakespeare CD-ROM: Macbeth* (HarperCollins *Interactive*/BBC/Attica Cybernetics).